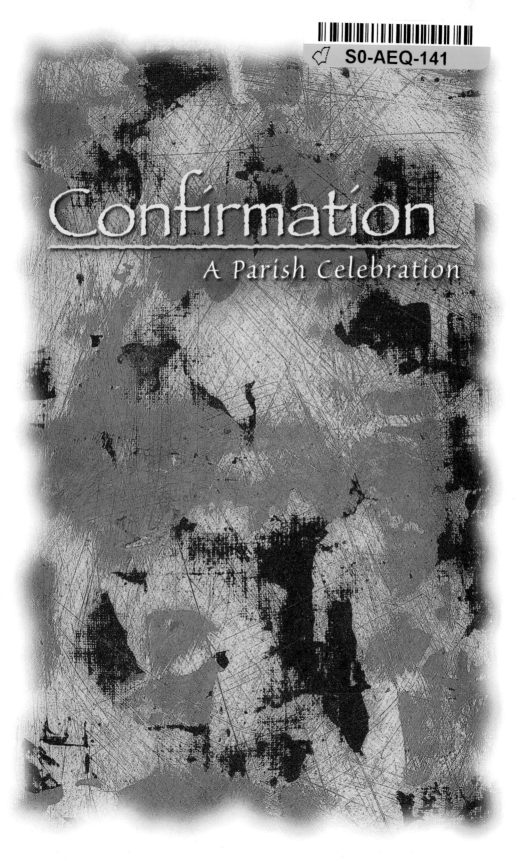

Confirmation

A Parish Celebration

Font and Table Series

The Font and Table Series offers pastoral perspectives on Christian baptism, confirmation and eucharist.

Other titles in the series:

A Catechumenate Needs Everybody: Study Guides for Parish Ministers
At That Time: Cycles and Seasons in the Life of a Christian
Baptism Is a Beginning
The Catechumenate and the Law
Celebrating the Rites of Adult Initiation: Pastoral Reflections
The Church Speaks about Sacraments with Children: Baptism,
*   Confirmation, Eucharist, Penance*
Confirmed as Children, Affirmed as Teens
Finding and Forming Sponsors and Godparents
Guide for Sponsors
How Does a Person Become a Catholic?
How to Form a Catechumenate Team
Infant Baptism: A Parish Celebration
Issues in the Christian Initiation of Children
One at the Table: The Reception of Baptized Christians
Readings in the Christian Initiation of Children
Welcoming the New Catholic

Related materials available through Liturgy Training Publications:

The Rite of Christian Initiation of Adults (ritual and study editions)
Rito de la Iniciación Cristiana de Adultos (ritual and study editions)
Catechumenate: A Journal of Christian Initiation
Baptism Sourcebook
Forum Essays series:
       The Role of the Assembly in Christian Initiation
       Eucharist as Sacrament of Initiation
       On the Rite of Election
       Preaching the Rites of Christian Initiation
       Liturgical Spirituality and the Rite of Christian Initiation of Adults

Confirmation

A Parish Celebration

Revised Edition

Timothy Fitzgerald

LITURGY
TRAINING
PUBLICATIONS

Acknowledgments

Excerpts from the English translation of Constitution on the Sacred
Liturgy, General Instruction of the Roman Missal, Rite of Confirmation,
General Introduction to Rite of Christian Initiation of Adults from
Documents on the Liturgy, 1963 –1979: Conciliar, Papal and Curial Texts © 1982
International Committee on English in the Liturgy, Inc.
All rights reserved.

Excerpts from Annibale Bugnini's *The Reform of the Liturgy, 1948 –1975*
© 1990. Used by permission of The Liturgical Press.

CONFIRMATION: A PARISH CELEBRATION, REVISED EDITION © 1999
Archdiocese of Chicago: Liturgy Training Publications, 1800 North
Hermitage Avenue, Chicago IL 60622-1101; 1-800-933-1800;
orders@ltp.org; fax 1-800-933-7094. All rights reserved.

This book was edited by Victoria M. Tufano. The production editor was
Bryan Cones. The book was designed by Peter Pona, and Jim Mellody-
Pizzato was the production artist. Cover and interior illustrations are by
Kris Hargis. The typefaces used in this book are Mrs. Eaves, Papyrus
and Sansvito. It was printed in Canada by Webcom Limited.

03 02 01 00 99   5 4 3 2 1

Library of Congress Cataloging-in-Publications Data
Fitzgerald, Timothy, 1947-
    Confirmation: a parish celebration / Timothy Fitzgerald. — Rev. ed.
        p.   cm. — (Font and table series)
    Includes bibliographical references.
    ISBN 1-56854-101-5
    1. Confirmation (Liturgy) 2. Confirmation — Catholic church.
    3. Catholic church — Liturgy. I. Title. II. Series.
    BX2210.F58   1999
    264'.02082— dc21   98-49840
                                                        CIP

CONF/R

Table of Contents

Introduction

In 1971, the *Rite of Confirmation* for the Roman Catholic
Church, which had been revised at the direction of
the Second Vatican Council, was promulgated. In 1983,
the first edition of *Confirmation: A Parish Celebration,* a
reflection upon our celebration of the rite, was first
published. Now, almost thirty years after the revised rite
appeared in English, and fifteen years after this book
appeared in its first version, we take another look at the rite
and our experience of it.

It's not that the rite itself has changed since 1971, but
that so much else has. Our pastoral practice of the rite,
indeed our pastoral experience with the whole of Christian
initiation, has changed dramatically. And our experience
of Christian initiation with those of catechetical age and
older continues to change at an amazing pace.

In 1971, catechumens were historical curiosities.
Now, they are a normal fixture of parish communities in
North America and many other parts of the world. Then,
the phrase "minister of initiation" meant the pastor.
Now, we talk about the many ministers of initiation, for the
coordinated efforts of many — catechists, preachers, sponsors,
hospitality teams, priests, pastoral ministers, liturgists,
musicians, religious educators and the assembly itself — have

become essential. Then, the physical presence of the bishop
was essential for confirmation in all but the rarest of
situations. Now, in many parishes the pastor or other presbyters routinely administer the sacrament at the Easter Vigil
or at other times during the liturgical year. Then, only
schooled liturgists and sacramental theologians suggested
that confirmation belonged before first communion,
not after, or that confirmation meant anything other than
becoming a soldier for Christ. Now, a growing number
of dioceses in English-speaking countries around the world
are celebrating confirmation before or at the same time
as first communion, and martial talk about confirmation
has been replaced by phrases such as "sacrament of
initiation" and "reiteration of baptism."

Many aspects of our liturgical life have also improved
since the first edition of this book was published. At that
time, it was necessary to remind parishes that the psalm was
to be sung and that the role of the cantor might be an
appropriate liturgical ministry. The practice of communion
from the cup was still irregular and often dropped from
the confirmation liturgy as too complicated or demanding.
Confirmation was often scheduled willy-nilly, even on
the First Sunday of Lent (in lieu of a diocesan rite of election) or on the Sunday of the Lord's Passion. In some
dioceses, confirmation was held in conjunction with bene-
diction rather than with celebration of the eucharist.

Today, the ministry of the cantor is recognized as a valuable enrichment to our prayer. Communion from the cup has again become a standard part of the liturgy in most parishes, after an absence of 800 years. Parishes and dioceses still contort matters to accommodate the bishop's schedule, but there is a much greater appreciation of the liturgical year and seasons than before. Parishes know better than they used to that celebrations of baptism or confirmation are not appropriate to the season of Lent. The robust celebration of the eucharist is taken as a given with the confirmation liturgy.

But it is more than that. Significant texts have influenced our pastoral liturgy and enriched our understanding. The provisional text of the *Rite of Christian Initiation of Adults,* in English since 1974 and in definitive form since 1988, lays out a model for initiation and the sacraments of initiation which is still instructing us. The *Ceremonial of Bishops,* published in English in 1989, reiterates many of the best perspectives from the church's ritual texts. Finally, the late Archbishop Annibale Bugnini's *The Reform of the Liturgy, 1948–1975* (Collegeville: The Liturgical Press, 1990) offers a detailed account of how the rite of confirmation was revised, including the many compromises that were forced upon it.

Other significant changes also have influenced the liturgy and our understanding of it. In the United States alone, catechumens and candidates for full communion number in the tens of thousands. The primary liturgy of initiation, the Easter Vigil, now presents us with a single ritual of initiation that moves from the waters of baptism to the laying on of hands and anointing, and only then to full participation in the assembly's gathering at table for the eucharist.

As our experience of confirmation changes, so our understanding of confirmation changes. Here is the simple conviction that animates this book. As we experience the whole of Christian initiation differently than we did thirty years ago, so our understanding of initiation has been affected. We experience — and therefore understand — confirmation differently than we did thirty years (or even fifteen years) ago. Do you want your diocese or your parish to understand Christian initiation or one dimension of it — confirmation — more fully? The best way to do this is to be sure the community's liturgies of initiation, including confirmation, are celebrated as fully and honestly as possible.

That is the goal of this simple book. It is meant to help pastoral and liturgical ministers examine the rite of confirmation in depth and detail, consider confirmation in the fuller context of Christian initiation, prepare the liturgy in full and honest fashion, and prepare the local community for its essential role as minister of the liturgy. The better we celebrate and experience the liturgy, the better we will understand the reality we celebrate.

Celebrating confirmation well will not resolve all the questions and issues swirling around it. Some of these issues simply will not go away. Archbishop Bugnini's account of the reform of the rite, prompted by the Second Vatican Council's *Constitution on the Sacred Liturgy*, will make you both smile and weep.

> The path of reform for the rite of confirmation was a long and difficult one because of the many problems . . . the uncertainties, and the diversity in theological and pastoral thinking about it. There were, and remain, questions about the connection of confirmation with baptism, a connection that the liturgy constitution had asked should be made to stand out more clearly; about the minister, the matter and form, the best age for reception; about the very meaning of the sacrament. . . . All these problems reared their heads, sometimes with passionate insistence, in the studies conducted by the Consilium and in the solutions proposed there.
>
> As early as the period when preparations were being made for the Council, some bishops had been asking that, above all else, answers be found to the question of the age of confirmation and the question of its minister. (*The Reform of the Liturgy, 1948–1975*, page 613; see Bugnini's entire chapter on the rite of confirmation, pages 613–625.)

Have some parishes transformed confirmation into
a "sacrament of required service hours" with a preparation
process more exacting and extensive than nearly anything else related to the sacraments? Have some parishes
trivialized "apostolic activity" into mundane tasks around
the parish property — raking leaves, washing windows,
cleaning the church? Have well-intentioned efforts to require
"mature commitment" for confirmation — a rationale for
delaying confirmation toward ages 15 to 18, as much as seven
to ten years after first communion — distorted confirmation into a graduation ceremony? Are we still expending
energy on the wrong questions? Is the rite more an exposition
of the person of the bishop than it ought to be? These
pastoral issues will be with us well into the new millennium.

Still, celebrating well the liturgy of confirmation — and
the whole of Christian initiation — does (and will) influence our understanding and our future practices. Already,
our fuller experience of Christian initiation is changing
our understanding of confirmation and effecting a further
change in our practice. In a growing number of dioceses
in Australia, New Zealand, Scotland and also the United
States, confirmation is now celebrated prior to or at the
same time as a child's first communion — a pastoral change
prompted in large part by changed experience of Christian
initiation, and thus a changed understanding.

A 1996 survey of dioceses in the United States about
the sacraments of initiation for children conducted by

the United States Catholic Conference Subcommittee on
Catechesis revealed this changing sacramental practice.
The subcommittee requested responses from all United States
dioceses, and then presented a summary report to the U.S.
Bishops' Committee on the Liturgy at its meeting in
June 1997. Though the subcommittee's primary concern
was catechetical, its report also provided information
about the sequence for the sacraments of initiation and thus
information about the sacrament of confirmation.

According to the 1996 survey, in 125 dioceses the typical
sequence for the sacraments of initiation with children
baptized as infants was baptism, then eucharist and finally
confirmation (most often in adolescence, anywhere between
ages 12 and 18). Presently, confirmation in adolescence
remains the primary practice in the dioceses
of this country.

However, another ten dioceses reported they had revised
the order of the sacraments of initiation for children.
In these ten dioceses, children receive the sacraments of
initiation in the order the rites call for — baptism, then
confirmation and finally eucharist. In all ten dioceses, this
traditional sequence had been reinstated between 1990
and 1996.

Finally, another 30 dioceses reported that revising the
order of the sacraments of initiation was under study.
Their responses meant a variety of things: in some cases,

the diocese was beginning to consider a revision, with a few parishes trying out this revised order; in other cases, the revision was soon to become standard diocesan practice after some or several years of consideration.

Clearly, our liturgical experience of initiation is changing our understanding of it, which in turn is changing our pastoral practice. This is the strength and the wisdom of the liturgy: It reveals to us the reality we celebrate.

Your parish cannot resolve all the issues about confirmation, and some of those issues are not yours to solve. But you can do something that will point the way to better understandings and so to better pastoral practice: Celebrate the liturgies of initiation, including confirmation, well. Carefully prepare the liturgy of confirmation for the parish — and even more carefully, the parish for the liturgy.

That is the best you can do, and that will be enough.

Chapter One
Three Generations

My grandmother was born in the spring of 1881, the only child in her family born in the United States. Her parents, both of solid Catholic background, made arrangements for her baptism at once. Three days after her birth, her father and godparents carried her to their small-town parish church in rural Iowa. Her mother did not consider making the six-mile trip by horse and buggy, nor was it expected that she would be present. My grandmother was baptized in a private ceremony, with the small gathering as witnesses. In April 1893, shortly after her twelfth birthday, she was confirmed. She took the name of her favorite saint as her confirmation name, and, accompanied by a different relative as her sponsor, she was sealed with chrism and proclaimed to be a soldier of Christ. It was on that occasion that she met the bishop of the diocese for the only time in her life.

In May 1895, after she turned 14 years of age and following serious preparation, she received communion for the first time. This solemn occasion was marked with a special dress, a special candle, both a parish and a family celebration, and even a photograph. It was truly a cele-bration of her coming-of-age, both in the sacramental life of the church and in her social community. This was the fulfillment of her baptismal life, her acceptance into the adult community. She was now old enough to share in the ban-quet of the Lord and to assume adult responsibilities in her family. This marked as well the end of her formal religious formation; it was up to her family and close-knit community to lead her in the proper practice of the faith.

My father was born in 1917. His parents immediately arranged for baptism, having asked relatives to be godparents long in advance. Two days after his birth, his father and his godparents took him to the parish church for the private ceremony, witnessed by the three relatives and performed by the parish priest. In May 1924, at the age of seven, my father received communion for the first time. No longer the coming-of-age ceremony that my grandmother knew, this novel practice of communion at such an early age nonetheless retained much of the pageantry of the previous generation. His new shirt and tie, the parish breakfast afterward and the family gathering later that day all served to mark this occasion as a major experience of faith for him and his community. In May 1929, at 12 years of age, my father was confirmed. This event absorbed some of the significance that had been attached to first communion in my grandmother's time. He was now "of age" in the church and in his family; the bishop himself welcomed my father as an adult witness for Christ. And now his formal religious education came to an end. Confirmation marked the end, literally, of his initiation into the church.

These two descriptions betray two quite different practices and theologies of Christian initiation. What happened to sacramental practice between my grandmother's childhood and that of my father has influenced the common practice to this day: the insightful call of Pope Pius X to welcome children to the eucharistic meal at an earlier age. Since then, those baptized as infants typically share in the eucharist for the first time around age eight and are confirmed between the ages of 12 and 18. In one motion, confirmation became what it had never been before: the end point of initiation, replacing eucharist as the climax of baptism. The consequences of that change are with us still, affecting our understanding of and approach to these sacraments.

More Changes

Today there are strong indications that this rather recent tradition in the life of the church may not remain as we know it. Pressures more profound than a papal directive are at work. Our experience and our catechetics suggest that something is not right. It is not just a question of reversing the order of first eucharist and confirmation again; it is more a question of how we have come to understand baptism, confirmation and eucharist in relation to each other.

Something new is happening. Over the past three decades parish assemblies have begun to experience the presence of catechumens in their midst. This is affecting the way we experience the sacraments, the liturgical year and the church itself. In addition, our practices surrounding infant baptism are changing: Infant baptism is more and more commonly a parish celebration. Add to this the fact that the documents of the church concerning sacraments consistently and deliberately speak about the sacraments of initiation

in this order: baptism, followed by confirmation, followed by eucharist. In the Apostolic Constitution on the
Sacrament of Confirmation, for example, the intention
to link confirmation with baptism and eucharist is
explicit: "The faithful are born anew by baptism, strengthened by the sacrament of confirmation, and finally are
sustained by the food of eternal life in the eucharist."
"Sacraments of initiation" and the "intimate connection
which confirmation has to the whole of Christian initiation" are discussed at great length both in the Apostolic
Constitution and in the Introduction to the *Rite of
Confirmation.* The documents imply two things: We cannot
understand these sacraments in their fullness except in
relation to each other; and we must understand these sacraments in this order and as a process, one leading to the next.

How is the practice of confirmation affected by all this?
Clearly, we cannot approach the celebration of confirmation as an isolated event. We are all too familiar with the
present variety of practices, perspectives, even theologies of
confirmation. Can we give this sacramental celebration
some consistent foundation?

The consistency must come by reconnecting confirmation with baptism and the eucharist in parish practice.
The rite of confirmation itself is filled with baptismal
language and baptismal symbolism. If we base our confirmation catechesis and liturgy firmly on baptism, and understand confirmation as leading to eucharist, then we can be

confident of our theological direction. As we rediscover
the rich and powerful symbolism of baptism, as we rediscover eucharist as the culmination of the sacraments of
initiation, we must necessarily rediscover confirmation not
as an end but as a transition, a step in the process of growth
into Christ. Confirmation has surely suffered from well-
intentioned attempts to make it the climax and high point
of Christian initiation — something that has no foundation
in our tradition. My grandmother's family perhaps did not
appreciate baptism as a public celebration of the faith of
the church and of birth into Christ as we do today. However,
they did appreciate, perhaps better than we do, that confirmation completes baptism and leads to the eucharistic
meal as the true fulfillment of the baptismal journey.
The social significance her family and community attached
to first eucharist has never transferred well to confirmation,
though we have certainly tried to do just that. Now we can
appreciate why this was never meant to be.

In time, our practices will change to conform to these
new insights and understandings. All the turmoil and
ferment having to do with initiation in our church is a birth
process, a purification, a sure sign of new growth. It is not
uncommon for our liturgical practice to lag behind our
theological insights. But just as surely, it is time now for good
liturgical experience to point the way toward reform. This
time the sacramental reforms can come about not as historical
afterthoughts, but as conscious steps to better express the
truth of our tradition: that "members of the living Christ

are incorporated into him and made like him through baptism, confirmation and the eucharist" (Vatican II, Decree on the Church's Missionary Activity, *Ad gentes,* 36).

Chapter Two

An Overview

I t will be helpful if you have a copy of the *Rite of Confirmation* at hand as you read this book; we will refer to it often. If you have not read the rite already, do so before reading any further. The rite is the essential starting point for planning the confirmation liturgy. A list of helpful resources is included in this book, but the chief guide for understanding confirmation and planning the liturgy is the *Rite of Confirmation* itself.

Key Elements Regarding Confirmation

As we look at the confirmation liturgy itself, it is important to keep firmly in mind certain elements about the sacrament: that it is a parish initiation liturgy; that it marks one stage of initiation; that what is sealed is not the candidate but the gift of the Spirit first given in baptism.

Confirmation Is a Parish Initiation Liturgy

The parish's celebration of confirmation is not an isolated event; it flows from and is related to the entire parish practice of initiation. Although the confirmation of those baptized as infants does not occur frequently in the parish, it is nevertheless part of the series of parish liturgies of initiation that take place during the year. It is related to the rites of the catechumenate and to the rite of election, which are parts of the process of Christian initiation for adults. It is also closely related to the primary parish initiation liturgy, the Easter Vigil, and to the celebrations of infant baptism and first eucharist. The confirmation liturgy, then, must be placed in the context of these other celebrations.

It is not proper to overdo this liturgy or to make it the grandest parish liturgy of the year.

Confirmation Marks One Stage of Initiation

Confirmation celebrates neither the beginning nor the end of Christian initiation for the candidates, but rather their gradual and continuing growth into the eucharistic community. With good reason, then, the rite strongly encourages us to celebrate confirmation in the context of the eucharist (*Rite of Confirmation,* 13; unless otherwise noted, all references are to the *Rite of Confirmation*). This helps us remember that eucharist, not confirmation, is the climax of the initiation process in the church. We are not celebrating a graduation in this liturgy, but growth in the baptismal way of life, which is meant to lead us all, including the candidates, into the eucharistic way of life throughout all our days. The candidates' growth into the living body of Christ is not finished by confirmation — it is only getting a good start.

What Is Sealed Is Not the Candidate

What is sealed in confirmation is the gift of the Spirit, poured out first of all upon the whole church, and also upon the candidates at baptism. Because of this, we need to avoid approaches to this liturgy that understand it either as a coming-of-age ritual or as a first-time reception of the Spirit. What we celebrate, seal, bless and make explicit by the celebration of confirmation is the presence of Christ's Spirit in our midst, that is, our common baptismal life.

The focus here is on the entire parish and its life in the Spirit, and the work that God has begun within us and among us in baptism.

The Rite of Confirmation within Mass

Now we can consider the rite of confirmation in a brief overview. In later chapters we will examine the elements of the rite and of the liturgical celebration in greater detail.

Entrance Rites

The opening moments of the liturgy of confirmation set the tone for the entire celebration. The procession of ministers, and perhaps of the candidates, is fittingly led by elements that announce this as an initiation liturgy: the Easter candle, a bowl of water for the rite of blessing and sprinkling holy water (unless the baptismal font can be used for this rite), and a large container of chrism. The book of the

scriptures and perhaps a bowl of burning incense might be
included in the procession as well. Accompanied by strong
and measured music, the procession focuses the attention of
all and announces this as a solemn and festive gathering.
The candle, water, chrism and incense are set in a prominent
place. The word is reverently placed for all to see. The
altar is reverenced, the sign of the cross is made and the
greeting is exchanged between presider and assembly.

Baptism is called to mind by the sprinkling rite,
which replaces the penitential rite. (The *Rite of Confirmation*
offers no suggestions about the entrance rite. This is
curious, since using the sprinkling rite seems so appropriate
and obvious in this liturgy.) The presider invites the assembly to pray together, then prays aloud in the name of all.
Having gathered together, proclaimed in word and action
our dignity as God's people, evoked our baptism by which
God forms us into the living Christ, and prayed with
one voice, we are then seated to give time and attention
to the scriptures.

Liturgy of the Word
The liturgy of the word for this liturgy needs close and
careful attention. By now we are familiar with the pattern
of silence, the word proclaimed, sung response. The other
necessities — quiet time for reflection, music both simple
and evocative, a cantor who engages the assembly in sung
prayer, a lector who strongly proclaims the scriptures —
are all woven together to fill our minds and hearts with the

spirit of the scriptures. This is the appropriate context in which to celebrate the life of God's Spirit in confirmation. "It is from the hearing of the word of God that the many-sided power of the Holy Spirit flows upon the church and upon each one of the baptized and confirmed, and it is by this word that God's will is manifest in the life of Christians" (#13).

Rite of Confirmation

From this liturgical context of evoking our baptism and encountering God's living word, the rite of confirmation then begins. Within the rite are six major actions, each needing careful forethought:

* Presentation of the candidates
* Homily or instruction
* Renewal of baptismal promises
* Laying on of hands
* Anointing with chrism
* General intercessions

The candidates are formally and publicly presented, each called by name. The homily opens up to them and the entire assembly the significance of this event. The candidates are then called upon to make a public profession of faith, as the adult community did when these candidates were baptized as infants. That baptismal faith now becomes explicit.

With prayer and song, and accompanied by repre-
sentatives of the community that sustains their baptismal
faith, the candidates have hands laid upon them and
are anointed with chrism, the perfumed "oil of gladness."
These strong and ancient gestures of inheritance and blessing
and invocation seal and make explicit the enduring pledge
of Christ: "The Spirit of truth will be with you." In this way,
the baptismal gift of the Spirit is sealed and the candidates
are brought more fully into the eucharistic community.

The rite of confirmation closes with prayer, the general
intercessions, through which we bring to the Lord the
needs of the church and of the whole world, asking God to
complete the growth in faith which God has begun and
which we celebrate by this rite.

Liturgy of the Eucharist
The entire liturgy finds its fulfillment in the liturgy of the
eucharist. Here is the sacred meal of the Risen Christ and
his anointed ones, the feast of the Spirit-filled people of
Christ. By sharing the scriptures we have called to mind the
covenant between God and the people. By the confirmation
of these candidates we have celebrated the continual
unfolding of that covenant. Now we join in the covenant
meal by which all the baptized and anointed reseal that
bond in Christ.

Rite of Confirmation outside Mass

The simpler rite of confirmation outside Mass has the same focus on initiation as the celebration within Mass. The emphasis here is likewise the candidates' continuing growth in Christ. Including the elements of initiation in the entrance procession (the candle, the water, the chrism) can highlight the baptismal nature of this celebration. Replacing the penitential rite with the sprinkling rite is helpful for properly celebrating confirmation as one of the sacraments of Christian initiation. The liturgy of the word forms the setting for the rite of confirmation; beginning with the sharing of the word reminds us that our covenant of faith exists because of God's initiative, not ours. Even if confirmation is celebrated outside Mass, "there should first be a celebration of the word of God" (#13).

After the word is proclaimed and heard, the confirmation rite itself is celebrated. Each of the six elements listed above needs the same careful planning. Following the general intercessions, all join in the Lord's Prayer. Each time we gather for the eucharist, we pray together this table prayer of the eucharistic community. At the rite of infant baptism outside Mass, all gather around the altar for the Lord's Prayer, a reminder of the day to come when the newly-baptized infant will be fully initiated into the body of Christ and will partake in the eucharistic meal. Praying this table prayer in this simpler celebration reminds us that confirmation, like baptism, finds its full meaning in the eucharist. It reminds us that Christian initiation is a process of growth into the eucharistic community, the dying-and-rising people who break bread together as the ultimate expression of its identity and mission. The rite of confirmation outside Mass concludes with the bishop's blessing (either in the form of a solemn blessing or a prayer over the people).

Why Celebrate Confirmation outside Mass?

The rite states that if the candidates have not yet received the eucharist and will not at this liturgy, or "if there are other special circumstances, confirmation should be celebrated outside Mass" (#13). This directive becomes a consideration as more dioceses restore the traditional order of the sacraments of initiation. When confirmation is celebrated before the candidates' sharing of eucharist, the confirmation liturgy may take place at the Mass at which the candidates also receive the eucharist for the first time. If the candidates' first communion will be delayed until another time, however, the confirmation liturgy takes place outside Mass.

Notice again that the rite (#13) assumes as the general practice that confirmation is celebrated prior to first communion and that the candidates are then admitted to the eucharist: "Christian initiation reaches its culmination in the communion of the body and blood of Christ. The newly confirmed therefore participate in the eucharist, which completes their Christian initiation." The celebration of confirmation outside the Mass is the exception rather than the rule.

The rite does not suggest or support the practice we have come to consider normal: first communion preceding confirmation by as much as ten years. The rite makes the cohesion and integrity of the sacraments of initiation a priority. Confirmation is intimately tied to eucharist so that "the fundamental connection of this sacrament with all of Christian initiation may stand out in clearer light" (*Constitution on the Sacred Liturgy,* 71). Neither confirmation nor eucharist is to be understood or practiced as an afterthought. Confirmation is the affirmation of our baptismal status and the entrance to the eucharistic table and eucharistic people. If those newly confirmed are not immediately led to the eucharistic table, then the eucharist is to be omitted. Otherwise, the liturgy at which those newly confirmed were not permitted to partake of communion would celebrate the exact opposite of the church's understanding that confirmation, springing from baptism, means entrance into eucharist.

In practice, the majority of those confirmed in the United States are already sharing in the eucharist at the time of their confirmation. Out of this confusing sacramental practice spring questions like, "Are they mature enough for confirmation yet?" But this is the wrong question, based as it is upon our distorted practice of separating eucharist from confirmation. Instead, the rite indicates that we should ask of our sacramental practice, "Why are they sharing in the eucharist if they have not been confirmed? How do we rationalize their sharing in the eucharist but refuse them confirmation for as much as a decade? How can they be mature enough for eucharist, but not mature enough for the sacrament which is meant to be the entrance to the eucharist?"

The proper celebration of confirmation is pointing us toward further reform and revision of our casual separation of eucharist and confirmation. If candidates already share in the eucharist, the presumption is that confirmation will take place at Mass and the candidates will continue to fully share in the eucharist. If candidates do not yet fully share in the eucharist, the rite presumes that the candidates will be confirmed and then receive the eucharist for the first time at that same liturgy, thus reiterating the essential unity of these sacraments of initiation. Otherwise, the candidates will be confirmed at the simpler liturgy, which does not include celebration of the eucharist. The rite's intention is to avoid the awkward situation of celebrating confirmation but then denying the newly confirmed access to the eucharist, one of the purposes of confirmation.

Chapter Three
Elements of Celebration

The Introduction to the *Rite of Confirmation* speaks repeatedly of two events: baptism and Pentecost. The one event, celebrated often in the life of the church, marks the ever-new birth of disciples into the life of Christ and into the life of the community. The other, the fulfillment of the risen Lord's promise, defines the community as the dwelling place of his Spirit for all time.

These two events, one repeated often and one unique to the formation of the church, shape confirmation for us. These related events echo throughout the language and symbolism of the confirmation rite. The symbols of the confirmation liturgy are drawn from this "water and the Spirit" history of the church; they are simple, ancient and strong. If the symbolic actions of confirmation are allowed to speak to us simply and clearly, as symbols are meant to, they will speak to us of baptism and Pentecost — which is exactly what they should do.

Actions

Historically, the sacrament of confirmation developed from the baptismal liturgy. Baptism is the source and foundation of confirmation's symbols and actions. Consider these actions from the confirmation rite and their parallels in the other rites of Christian initiation.

* *Presentation of the Candidates:* similar to the rite of becoming a catechumen or the rite of election; similar to the reception of the child in infant baptism

* *Renewal of Baptismal Promises:* taken directly from the baptismal rite

* *Laying on of Hands:* the gesture of invoking the Spirit, repeated often with the catechumens; also in the baptism of infants (if the infants are not anointed with the oil of catechumens)

* *Anointing with Chrism:* an integral part of sacraments of initiation with catechumens, also part of the baptism of infants

It is this baptismal nature, this initiatory character of the confirmation liturgy, that needs to be enhanced. This requires that careful thought and planning go into the liturgy, its objects and its symbolic actions.

Obvious, full, uncluttered, visible, simple — these words should describe both the objects we use in our rites and the actions in which we employ them. We need to give careful attention well in advance to the water used to evoke baptism, and the chrism by which we are anointed in the Spirit. These primary elements of the rite of confirmation are accompanied by others: the Easter candle, given prominence at the Easter Vigil and all other parish initiation liturgies; the book of the scriptures, carried in procession and given proper reverence; the plate of bread and decanter of wine, the food and drink for the eucharistic meal.

Water

Our journey as part of the living body of Christ begins with baptism. The baptismal water and its use in the sprinkling rite can help frame and define the confirmation liturgy. The words of blessing over these waters of death and resurrection and the sprinkling of the assembly can announce clearly that Christian life begins with baptism. Even the baptismal font can figure in the liturgy, if it is in plain view. The Easter candle and chrism might be carried there after the entrance procession, and the blessing of the water, which begins the sprinkling rite, can take place at the font.

For parish communities that have a prominent font in their worship space, the font becomes for them a holy site, an icon of God's action in the assembly's midst. The bridal couple blesses each other with water there at the beginning of the wedding liturgy. The body of the deceased is brought to be sprinkled by family members there as the funeral liturgy begins. The font is a focal point during the Easter season, the source and sign of baptisms present and past. The font is the starting point of this initiatory liturgy as well.

If the baptismal font is not easily accessible or not a good focal point, then a sizable container of water might be included in the entrance procession. This vessel can be carried during the sprinkling rite and then set in a prominent place, on a small table or stand, perhaps grouped with the Easter candle and chrism. One or several candles placed on the table with a plant or flowers, a bowl of burning incense set on the floor nearby, can provide a proper setting and highlight these fundamental elements of Christian initiation. Light and water and oil speak to us of our common life as the holy and anointed people of Christ.

Chrism

The Introduction to the Rite of Blessing of Oils and Consecrating the Chrism (see the sacramentary, appendix II) describes chrism as "made of oil and perfumes or other sweet smelling matter" (#4). The distinguishing trait of chrism is that it is perfumed, and this needs to be obvious whenever it is used.

Do some investigating: Find and purchase a perfumed oil to mix with the chrism for your parish. Oil-based perfume will mix well with the chrism; water-based perfume will not. Laudate Chrism Essence, available from Holy Rood Guild, 167 N. Spencer Rd., Spencer, MA 01562-1233, is a fine scent for the chrism. The time you spend on this detail will be well worth it.

The anointing with chrism is the sacramental sign of being consecrated to Christ, of one marked as a member of the community of the redeemed. The oil reflects the joy of the kingdom; its sweet, strong scent radiates from those anointed to permeate the whole gathering. That someone has been anointed on the forehead cannot be easily seen but ought to be obvious to our noses. Oftentimes the chrism supplied to the parish does not have a distinctive, perfumed scent, and smells just like the oil of the sick or the oil of the catechumens. Be sure to remedy this before the chrism is used.

Common sense should prevail in our approach to symbols. Obtain enough chrism for it to be substantial, full, obvious and visible. A plastic medicine bottle of chrism may be enough to "get the job done," but that amount is certainly unacceptable for it to be a full and visible symbol. Be sure the diocese provides you with enough chrism to fill a sizable container. Then when the anointing occurs there can be a liberal use of the chrism, so that the oil and its scent will be striking to the candidates and to the entire assembly. It is the sign that the one anointed has been united with Jesus the Christ, "the anointed one of the Lord," and such a sign should be richly used.

It is certainly appropriate that the chrism be carried in procession, then placed in a fitting and visible spot to be enhanced throughout the liturgy by the reverence and care with which it is surrounded. This presupposes a container that is sizable, simple and elegant. A large, clear container made of cut glass or crystal works very well: The oil is visible to all and the container is suitably dignified. Because the chrism will be poured from this container into smaller bowls for the anointing, the container should allow the oil to be poured easily.

Easter Candle

The Easter candle can also serve as a prominent fixture for the liturgy. If it is of manageable size, it can be carried in procession, then placed near the water and chrism or set by the font (its proper place throughout the year). Many parishes now use a large Easter candle that is not easily carried or moved about. This larger candle could simply be left in place, but made prominent with plants or flowers around the base and burning brightly for all to see. It is an exceedingly appropriate object to highlight for confirmation, since the celebration is an initiation liturgy.

Other Items

Contrary to popular opinion, it is possible to celebrate the rite of marriage without the lighting of a unity or Christ

candle. It is a sentimental touch, and some veiled significance can be drawn from the newlyweds jointly lighting
a candle, but it is not part of the official rite. In some ways
it clutters the exchange of commitment.

Two such items have similarly grown up around the rite
of confirmation: candles and "confirmation stoles." They
likewise are nice, homey touches added to the rite. Though
their significance may seem more obvious than a unity candle at a wedding, they just as easily qualify as clutter.
Giving each confirmation candidate a candle lit from the
Easter candle and placing a decorated "confirmation stole"
around his or her neck are extra efforts to evoke the baptismal nature of this celebration. They are derived from the
rite of baptism itself: from the clothing with the baptismal
garment and the lighting of the baptismal candle from
the Easter candle.

But confirmation is an expansion of baptism, not
a repeat of it. The baptismal garment, proper to the baptismal liturgy, is meant to be a true garment, not reduced
to a bib or something that looks like a stole. To give a newly
baptized infant or adult a stole in place of a baptismal garment is, at best, a confusing gesture; and to reiterate or
even introduce this confusion at confirmation only compounds the matter. Is there any overwhelming reason to
introduce the baptismal garment or an allusion to it into
this liturgy?

Lighting candles from the Easter candle is proper to the annual Easter Vigil, the service that is precisely a celebration and renewal of everyone's baptism. We don't want to imitate baptism at the confirmation liturgy, as if it were so weak that we need every possible allusion to baptism in order to rescue it. There are more authentic ways to emphasize the initiatory context of confirmation: beginning the liturgy with the rite of blessing and sprinkling holy water, ensuring the presence of parish catechumens and neophytes, and making the renewal of baptismal promises a strong ritual moment.

Chapter Four

Ritual Words and Actions

We tend to ignore the series of processions, the movement of people and objects, that mark our liturgies. Usually these processions occur with little thought or rehearsal, in part because they have become so familiar to us when we gather for prayer. For the confirmation liturgy, however, even these familiar processions — of the ministers, the gospel book, the gifts for the eucharist, the assembly — may be unusual. The entrance procession, for instance, might include the candidates with their sponsors or parents; the preparation of the altar and procession with the gifts might involve some of the newly confirmed. For this liturgy, even these familiar processions require forethought.

In addition, the movement of people during the rite of confirmation itself requires close attention and thought. This obliges the planners to understand the rite, to remember its focus and its priorities. The rite begins after the proclamation of the gospel, before the homily. Some of the processions and movements of the rite of confirmation are sketched out below.

Presentation of the Candidates

After the gospel reading, the candidates are presented.

> If possible, each . . . is called by name and comes individually to the sanctuary. If . . . children, they are accompanied by one of their sponsors or parents and stand before the celebrant. (*Rite of Confirmation* [RC], 21)

32

They move forward "to a suitable place," or at least stand in place while everyone else remains seated.

The parallels to our other rites of initiation are obvious. At the rite of acceptance into the order of catechumens, the inquirers are literally called into the assembly, called by name to declare their desire to be part of the church. At the rite of election, the catechumens are called forward publicly so their names may be included in the book of the elect. Their election by God for the sacraments of the church is reflected in this public presentation. At the baptism of children, the presider formally asks the parents what the children are to be called, then calls the children by name to claim them as followers of Jesus Christ.

Similarly, at confirmation the candidates are called forth by name, one at a time. They do not present themselves; they are called forth. They come to confirmation not as a testimony of their action but as a reminder of God's action. This ritual moment thus reflects the truth of all Christian initiation: The initiative does not rest with the individuals.

That is why those called forth take a prominent place as the focus of attention for the bishop and the entire assembly (RC, 21). They may even remain standing during the brief homily to follow. That the candidates have been led to this point is a testimony to the faith and commitment of parents, family and parish, animated by God's initiative.

The candidates stand in the midst of the assembly as living witness to God's action, not to their own accomplishments, as icons of the Spirit of Christ moving and acting with the church. It is a brief glimpse of the truth, to be cherished by all who take part in and witness it, that when God's word is proclaimed the church is built up in faith and communion.

The homily follows. The presentation of the candidates can be a rich starting point for the brief homily: God is calling these candidates to growth in faith and service, a flesh-and-blood sign in our midst that God is calling the entire church to growth in faith and service. If the candidates have moved forward when called by name, they might remain standing for the homily. If they stood in place near their families and sponsors, they could be seated.

Renewal of Baptismal Promises

If the candidates were seated for the homily, they now stand for the renewal of baptismal vows. This moment has parallels in other initiation liturgies. At the baptism of children, the church proclaims its faith, the shared belief and meaning that is the context for the ritual actions. The assembly, the parents and the godparents renounce evil and profess their faith. The adult community proclaims its belief about what is at stake. Even before the infants are aware of this, the community is forming them in faith.

At the Easter Vigil, the elect profess faith publicly for the first time, then are brought into the sacramental life of the church. Sponsored and supported to this point, they now must state "our faith, the faith of the church" (*Rite of Baptism for Children* [RBC],59) on their own in order to come into the eucharistic people.

In parallel fashion, the candidates for confirmation now must state "our faith, the faith of the church" on their own, in their own name. They alone stand for this renewal and they alone respond to the questions.

Laying On of Hands

The imposition of hands is one of the most common of our sacramental gestures, and one of the most ancient and powerful. It is part of the rite of baptism for children; practiced throughout the rites of adult initiation by the many ministers of initiation; part of the prayer of absolution in the rite of penance; an integral part of the anointing of the sick; central to the ordination liturgy. The extension of hands occurs in the eucharistic prayer when we pray "let your Spirit come upon these gifts," and is proper to any of the solemn blessings or prayers over the people at the end of Mass. This gesture embodies blessing, compassion, unity. It denotes solemnity and consecration, and symbolizes God blessing the people and objects.

The Apostolic Constitution on the Sacrament of Confirmation (found in the front of the rite itself) recounts the history of the imposition of hands and the anointing with chrism as parts of the rite of confirmation, then opts for the anointing as the "essence of the sacramental rite." But the Apostolic Constitution also says that the laying on of hands is to be "held in high esteem, in that it contributes to the integral perfection of that rite and to a clearer understanding of the sacrament." The *Rite of Confirmation* itself says "the laying on of hands . . . is the biblical gesture by which the gift of the Holy Spirit is marked" (#9). This powerful gesture of the initiation rites is as histori- cally and scripturally significant to confirmation as is the anointing which follows. (The Apostolic Constitution explains at great length why the anointing is to be the primary ritual gesture, attempting to clarify the earlier rite, which literally prescribed that the laying on of hands and the anointing were to occur simultaneously — the bishop's hand imposed on the candidate's head while the bishop then used the thumb of the same hand to anoint the forehead.)

Whatever the history, the liturgy of confirmation is strengthened and enhanced if the assembly is first called to pray for the outpouring of the Spirit ("Let us pray . . . that God will pour out the Holy Spirit . . ."); and then, in real and deliberate fashion, hands are imposed upon the candidates. The prayer by the bishop ("Send your Holy Spirit upon them . . .") and the anointing itself are supported — not overshadowed — when hands are imposed upon each and all the candidates (though the rite allows that hands may be extended over the candidates as a group). This means that either the candidates will move toward the ministers for the imposition of hands or the ministers will move to where the candidates are standing (#6). (This laying on of hands need not be lengthy if, as the rite clearly assumes [#8], the presbyters are assisting the bishop.) The most obvious movement would be for the candidates, already standing because of the renewal of baptismal vows, to process to one of the ministers of confirmation, then process back to their places for the bishop's prayer which follows. Another model is for the ministers ("the bishop and the priests who will minister the sacrament with him" [#25]) to process to the candidates; the candidates remain with family members and sponsors while a minister approaches each candidate to impose hands. The candidates may even move into the aisles for this laying on of hands, which may be simplest if the number of candidates is large.

If it is impossible to arrange for the ministers to impose hands on the candidates individually, a good alternative is for the sponsors and/or parents to lay their hands on the candidates while the ministers extend hands over all. This ancient prayer gesture is thus expanded into the assembly itself.

With careful thought, this ancient gesture can be enhanced and will, in turn, greatly enhance the rite. The pattern would be: the bishop's call to prayer; silent prayer by all; a laying on of hands during more silence; the invocation of the Spirit, sung by the bishop.

Anointing

The anointing with chrism is associated with baptism, confirmation and ordination to the priesthood. It is the gesture that speaks of service and discipleship, of commitment and birthright. It is the mark of the kingdom. "When [those baptized] are anointed with this holy oil, make them temples of your glory. . . . Let this be indeed the chrism of salvation for those who will be born again of water and the Holy Spirit" (sacramentary, Consecration of the Chrism, 25).

The anointing at confirmation originates from the bishop (RC, 26). The container of chrism is brought from its place of prominence to the bishop, who pours a portion of the chrism into one or more small bowls. When priests assist in the anointing, they each come to the bishop to receive a vessel of chrism from him (#28).

Though the *Rite of Confirmation* contains no explicit reference to the chrism, a simple prayer of thanksgiving could be said as the chrism is poured into the small containers or immediately before the bishop and other ministers move to their places for the anointing. A portion of one of the prayers for the consecration of chrism (see the sacramentary, Rite of the Blessing of Oils and Consecrating the Chrism) could be adapted for this purpose. For example:

Father, you have made this mixture of oil and perfume a sign and source of your blessing. Let the splendor of holiness shine on the world from every person signed with this oil.

The chrism is not reconsecrated by this brief thanksgiving, and any adaptation of the prayer of consecration should be carefully worded to avoid that impression.

A precedent for this brief prayer occurs in the rite of the anointing of the sick (*Pastoral Care of the Sick*, 123). If the oil of the sick was blessed prior to the liturgy, a prayer of thanksgiving is to be said before the actual anointing. In similar fashion, the preparing and distributing of the blessed chrism at the confirmation liturgy might be accentuated by a brief acclamation of thanksgiving about the oil and its use.

The anointing is to be deliberate and obvious. A generous portion of the perfumed oil is smeared on the candidate's forehead in the shape of the cross, with the words, "N., be sealed with the Gift of the Holy Spirit." The oil is left on the forehead for all to see and smell, for this anointing is the mark of the baptized, signifying the church's birthright as the dwelling place of the Spirit. It designates those con-secrated to God as the new and holy people, in the tradition of the priests, prophets and kings of Israel, and of Jesus, the Anointed One.

The anointing requires the movement of those people immediately involved: candidates, sponsors, ministers. One option is for the ministers to move to one spot and the candidates to approach them (like the assembly approaches the ministers of communion). This is the typical practice for the anointing, but there are other options. The anointing, like the laying on of hands, need not be confined to the front of the worship space. The ministers can move through the aisles to the candidates and sponsors, anointing the candidates who are standing with or near their sponsors and family members.

At first glance, this option may seem unworkable. But many parishes now routinely perform some of the rituals of adult initiation in ways that never used to occur to us. For example, during the rite of acceptance into the order of catechumens, the first questioning and welcoming occur outside the worship space or in the doorway. In the same rite, the signing of the senses often proceeds with cate-chumens and sponsors standing in the aisles, literally in the midst of the assembly. In the scrutiny rites during Lent, the elect and godparents are easily situated in the aisles for prayer and the imposition of hands.

We used to assume that all liturgical actions needed to take place in or near the sanctuary to be legitimate. Now we are beginning to understand that the place of the assembly is also a hallowed and holy setting, and that some ritual actions are better situated in the midst of the assembly than in front of it. Perhaps this is the case with the confirmation rite's laying on of hands and anointing. If these ritual actions take place in the assembly rather than in front, if the ministers move rather than the candidates and sponsors, will the rituals be more evocative and accessible than before? Will people thus experience confirmation in a better way and so be helped to understand confirmation in a better way? Will this simplify arrangements for moving people during the rite of confirmation? We won't know until we try it, will we?

Chapter Five
Liturgy of the Word

I n all the sacramental revisions mandated by Vatican II,
one principle was followed very closely: First comes
a sharing of the scriptures, and then the sacramental
actions. Whether in the celebration of marriage, of
reconciliation, of anointing of the sick, or of confirmation, the good news is first proclaimed and reflected
upon. Only then do we express our response of faith by
our sacramental actions.

These actions, and our lives of faith which they epitomize,
are set firmly on the foundation of the word proclaimed
and listened to, prayed over and acted upon. The sacraments are not isolated events or independently empowered.
All of the sacraments are to be understood and celebrated
within this context: Our faith is a response to the good news
of God's love.

Our basic understanding of confirmation, our theology of this sacrament of initiation, is going to affect
our approach to the liturgy of the word. A reading does
not have to mention explicitly the Holy Spirit in order
to be a legitimate selection; confirmation is not the only
or even the primary celebration of the gift of Christ's
Spirit. The readings have more to do with beginnings and
new life than with farewells; confirmation is not a graduation or the end of a journey.

The readings lead us to reflect upon our communal life
in Christ rather than on the worthiness of the candidates;

confirmation is a celebration of the community's baptismal life, not the awarding of a spiritual merit badge. A Holy Spirit theme is certainly not the sole factor in selecting the readings. Our approach to confirmation, which is embodied in and flows from the scriptures, involves baptism, the journey of Christian initiation, the dying-and-rising life of Christ's disciples, the community as the dwelling place of his Spirit. These are the reflections we bring to the planning of the word service; our insights will be blessed and multiplied as we spend time with the readings. The little with which we begin will be expanded and enriched by the living word long before the liturgy itself. The planning for the entire liturgy will necessarily start with the word service. In order of priority, formation of the liturgy of the word involves

* selection of the gospel reading
* selection of the first reading
* selection of the psalm and refrain
* selection of a second reading
* selection of a verse before the gospel

Three readings may be selected (as with the lectionary for Sundays and major feasts) or two readings (as with the lectionary for weekdays). The important consideration is that the word service enable the assembly to feast on the scriptures. This can be served well by the use of two readings. Including more than two readings does not necessarily ensure a better experience (see *Directory for Masses* with *Children*, 42–44). The competence of the lector, the pauses for reflection, the singing of the psalm and the quality of the preaching all affect the significance of the word service more than the number of readings.

The Readings

Sometimes we make our preparations for the confirmation liturgy more complicated than necessary. We set about constructing the liturgy of the word from scratch, which is not what the rite has in mind. In fact, the rite points to a simpler approach that we seldom utilize.

Start with the Lectionary

The *Rite of Confirmation* (#20) suggests that our starting point be the lectionary's readings for the particular day or week that confirmation will take place. These might be supplemented or amended with readings suggested for rite of confirmation. "The readings may be taken in whole or in part from the Mass of the day or from the texts for confirmation in the *Lectionary for Mass* (nos. 763–767)."

There is a certain wisdom in starting with the lectionary. It teaches us that celebrating the sacraments of initiation is better suited to some times of the church year than others. For instance, the Sunday and weekday readings for the season of Easter overflow with the language, images and concerns of communal life in Christ, strongly suggesting the Easter season for celebrating the sacraments of new life. In contrast, the readings for the season of Lent are filled with stories, images and language of conversion and repentance, since Lent exists to prepare the catechumens for baptism and to call the church back to its baptismal vows. The lectionary reminds us that Lent is not appropriate for confirmation or the other sacraments of Christian initiation.

Finally, the readings for the weeks of Ordinary Time often suit the confirmation liturgy. In fact, four of the gospel passages suggested for confirmation appear as Sunday readings:

* Matthew 5:1–12 (Fourth Sunday, Year A)
* Matthew 16:24–27 (Twenty-second Sunday, Year A)
* Matthew 25:14–30 (Thirty-third Sunday, Year A)
* Mark 1:9–11 (Baptism of the Lord, Year B)

The lectionary suggests that the Sundays of Ordinary Time may be well suited to a parish celebration of confirmation, and that we may need to look no further than the lectionary readings of that Sunday for the scriptures of the confirmation liturgy.

The *Ceremonial of Bishops* notes further that if confirmation is celebrated on a more important day of the church year — including the Sundays of Advent, Lent or Easter, within the octave of Easter, or on Epiphany, Ascension or Pentecost — "the Mass of the day, with its readings" are the texts to be used (see *Ceremonial of Bishops*, 459, and appendix II). This reiterates to planners the importance of attending to the lectionary and the calendar when preparing for this and other sacramental celebrations of the parish community.

In other words, the best way to begin planning the liturgy of the word for confirmation is to consult the liturgical calendar and the lectionary. The path of discipleship that leads from the font to the table, from the eucharistic food to the eucharistic people, from the table for eucharist to the world as eucharist — this is the heart of our gatherings week after week, season after season, year-in and year-out. We need not start from scratch for this parish liturgy of initiation, and the readings of Sunday may well provide one or more readings for this liturgy. Better for this liturgy to spring from the calendar and the lectionary of our church than to appear as if unrelated to either. Thus the rite again suggests a context for the celebration of confirmation: the regular worship of the parish community.

Selecting the Readings

To start the planning, read the readings and pray with them. Make notes about them, talk about them with others. Certainly the candidates can be reflecting on these readings, and their insights need to be solicited. What is it that these readings express? Why is this particular reading a good choice or not? Which readings speak most clearly about our common life as Christ's living body? What we ponder in these readings is nothing less than the central mystery of our discipleship: the unmerited unity with Christ of those who believe in him, sealed forever by his Spirit. Indulge yourselves in the planning process, and spend time touching the power of these readings. Then remember this is the goal of the word service as a whole: that the entire assembly encounter again the living spirit of the Lord, who has come "to live in our hearts and make us temples of his glory" (RC, 58). No matter which readings you select for the liturgy, spend time with them. Our study and contemplation of the readings guarantee a more profound liturgical experience.

Besides the readings of the day, week or season, consider other scripture readings suggested for the celebration of confirmation (#61−65). Twelve gospel readings are listed, twelve from the Acts of the Apostles and the letters, five from the Hebrew scriptures, and six psalms with seven responses. The possible combinations are numerous.

The proclamation of the gospel is the climax of the liturgy of the word. Because it forms the cornerstone of the entire liturgy of the word, it should be selected first. The twelve suggested gospel passages provide a wealth of material suited to confirmation. Consider the imagery and wisdom that flow from them: the Beatitudes, the "inaugural address of the kingdom" (Matthew 5:1−12); the cost of discipleship (Matthew 16:24−27); service to the Master and commitment to our mission (Matthew 25:14−30); the baptism of Jesus (Mark 1:9−11); Jesus' proclamation of Isaiah's prophecy concerning the Messiah (Luke 4:16−22); seeds of faith growing to maturity (Luke 8:4−10, 11−15); the manifesting of what had been hidden (Luke 10:21−24);

nourishment from the Lord (John 7:37–39); discipleship
sustained by the Spirit (John 14:15–17; John 14:23–26);
the consolation and vindication for the faithful ones by
the Spirit of the risen Lord (John 15:18–21, 26–27; John
16:5–7, 12–13).

If two readings are chosen to accompany the gospel, the
first is taken from the Hebrew Scriptures and the second
from the New Testament. If only one reading is to be proclaimed before the gospel, any of these suggested readings
from the Hebrew Scriptures, Acts of the Apostles or epistles
may be chosen. The possible readings include imagery of
the Suffering Servant from Isaiah (Isaiah 42:1–3),
accounts of powerful visions from Ezekiel and Joel (Ezekiel
36:24–28; Joel 2:23; 3:1–3), passages from Acts about
Christ's Spirit lavishly poured out (like anointing oil) on
the early believers (Acts 2:1–6, 14, 22–23, 32–33), and
some of Saint Paul's finest reflections on the significance
of it all (for example, Romans 5:1–2, 5–8).

The Psalm

The psalm and its antiphon (refrain) are chosen to provide
a reflection on and enhancement of the first reading; it
also serves as a link between this reading and the gospel. The
psalms listed in the rite (#63) emphasize the grandeur of
God, God's reign over all creation, the thanksgiving due for
God's glorious deeds, and the justice and righteousness
flowing from God's love. They are beautiful prayers of an

awestruck and grateful people, certainly appropriate for the confirmation liturgy.

Or we might take our cue from the lectionary, which provides for a psalm and response throughout a particular season (#174). The psalm and response at the confirmation liturgy might be the same one the parish is using throughout the Easter season, for example, Psalm 118 with "This is the day the Lord has made; let us rejoice and be glad"; or Psalm 66 with "Let all the earth cry out to God with joy." During the Easter season it is always appropriate to sing "alleluia" as the response with the psalm (see the lectionary, #173–174, for the suggested common psalms and responses).

It cannot be stated often enough that the psalm is meant to be sung. Once the psalm and antiphon are chosen, planners and musicians can then select the musical setting. The problem will not be finding a good and suitable musical setting of the psalm, but choosing from among the many possibilities.

The Gospel Acclamation and Verse

A gospel acclamation sung by cantor and congregation is part of the dynamic of the entire word service, part of the listening and responding pattern upon which the word service is built. It is not to be recited. If the gospel acclamation is used, it is to be sung; if it cannot be sung, it is omitted.

If this parish celebration is scheduled during Lent (which still occurs in a dwindling number of parishes and dioceses), remember that "alleluia" is not used. In Lent we substitute a seasonal gospel acclamation, such as "Glory and praise to you, Lord Jesus Christ." "Alleluia," the glorious acclamation of the Easter mystery, is saved until the Vigil.

The Lector

At a liturgical convention some years ago, a large crowd gathered on the last day for a glorious celebration of the eucharist. An assembly eager to participate, a choir and small orchestra with hand bells and pipe organ, excellent cantors, original music and artwork all made the liturgy a profoundly moving experience. But the most electrifying moment belonged to the lector.

Stepping to the platform in the center of the assembly, she stood proudly and quietly by the large Easter candle until the entire assembly grew silent. Then she boldly and deliberately proclaimed the reading from Isaiah. Her presence, her attitude, her voice, her preparedness commanded attention, and the thousands present reached for her every word. That reading was not casually handed to us — it was unveiled for us, and it enveloped us. Because of her, the words were absolutely spellbinding, and it was indeed Isaiah proclaiming the Lord's message of hope to us.

Would that every lector, every proclamation of the readings, could touch our hearts that deeply! Even if the setting is less elaborate and the liturgy more ordinary, there is no excuse for a lector to be incompetent, unprepared, inaudible or, worst of all, timid. Our goal is to have the assembly at the confirmation liturgy, or any liturgy, reach for every word from the lector's mouth. The lector more than anyone else has the power to bring the liturgy of the word to life or put the congregation to sleep. As we choose the readings for confirmation with care, so we should choose the lector with care.

Choosing Lectors

Who should proclaim the scriptures for this liturgy? Some would say one of the candidates' parents, since by baptism parents are called to "be the first and the best teachers of their children in the ways of faith" (*Rite of Baptism for Children,* 70). Some would say a godparent, since god-parents are involved in confirmation to "express more clearly the relationship between baptism and confirmation" (RC, 5) and since they represent the commitment of the community to the candidates. Some would choose one of the catechists, as a sign of their importance in forming the candidates and in helping "the seed [which] is the word of God" grow in their hearts and lives. Some would say one of the regular lectors of the parish should proclaim the word for this important parish liturgy. Some choose one from the most recent group of candidates confirmed in the parish, and some parishes even used to choose one of the candidates as lector. These last two practices have fallen out of favor, since they tend to convey a "graduation" approach to confirmation. Further, the candidates' par-ticipation as candidates is so important that they should not be asked to fill another ministerial role.

When choosing lectors for this liturgy, more important than questions of age, relationship to the candidates, experience as a lector or gender, are the questions of com-petence, articulation, ability to command attention and the living witness given to hearing the word and putting it into practice.

The scriptures can better come alive for us all if we choose and prepare the lector as conscientiously as we choose and prepare the readings. Further, the rapport between the

assembly and the word will be greatly enhanced if the
readings are not printed in a worship booklet. The proclamation of the scriptures is the public announcement of
God's action then and now, not a collective reading exercise.

The Homily

The readings for the confirmation liturgy and results of the
reflection upon them by candidates, catechists and planners
can be forwarded to the bishop far enough in advance to
help him in preparing the homily. Developing a fresh homily
for every confirmation can be a cross for the bishop to bear,
and often it becomes a burden upon the assembly as well.
The sample homily in the rite (#22) only compounds the
problem, encompassing as it does several theologies of
confirmation in seven short paragraphs. Often the homilist
resorts to presenting a history of confirmation, an overview
of salvation history, the role of the bishop as chief pastor,
a review of the Spirit in the scriptures, a pep talk on
Christian witness, an exhortation for frequent reception
of the sacraments or a plug for religious vocations — all
while calming everyone's fears about the bishop quizzing
the candidates.

Part of the problem stems from our pastoral practice
of confirmation. The excessive expectations on this
homily are symptoms of larger pastoral and sacramental
problems. In practice the confirmation liturgy is not
a parish celebration of initiation but a visit-of-the-bishop
liturgy. It remains more an episcopal liturgy than an

initiation liturgy, and usually the preaching is an exposition of the ministry of bishop rather than of Christian
initiation. If the minister of confirmation were the pastor
or another designated presbyter, the preaching might
very well improve, not because bishops are terrible preachers
or because the local presbyters are golden-tongued, but
because the focus would be more clearly on the liturgy
instead of the minister.

Further, the bishop is usually such an infrequent visitor
to a parish community that this liturgy and homily take
on far more significance than they can bear. The role of the
bishop in the life of the parish typically is exercised from a
distance and only in written form. The confirmation liturgy
tends to be his single pastoral visit for the entire year (or
longer). The bishop, the planners and the assembly expect
this homily to make up for what is lacking in pastoral
practice. Everything that could and should be said by the
bishop about the church and the life of the parish falls to
this one homily, stretching it to the breaking point.

The rite says simply, "The bishop then gives a brief
homily. He should explain the readings, and so lead [all] to
a deeper understanding of the mystery of confirmation"
(#22). One step in the right direction is to heed the word
brief and to rediscover that the liturgy itself preaches.
Besides, the readings are not the only starting point for a
homily. If we Catholics have rediscovered that preaching

has something to do with the scriptures, we have perhaps forgotten that preaching has something to do with the liturgical experience. In the Catholic tradition preaching is grounded in the scriptures *proclaimed in the liturgy.*

> That the intimate connection between words
> and rites may be apparent in the liturgy . . .
> the sermon should draw its content mainly from
> scriptural and *liturgical sources.* Its character should
> be that of a proclamation of God's wonderful
> works in the history of salvation, that is, the mystery
> of Christ, which is ever made present and active
> within us, especially in the celebration of the liturgy.
> (*Constitution on the Sacred Liturgy,* 35; emphasis added)

> The homily . . . should develop some point of the
> readings or of *another text from the [liturgy].* The homilist
> should keep in mind the mystery being celebrated
> and the needs of the particular community. (*General
> Instruction of the Roman Missal,* 41; emphasis added)

The liturgical texts and experience provide a wealth of starting points for the homily, evocative ways to "lead [all] to a deeper understanding of the mystery of confirmation." Why do we restate our baptismal vows at this liturgy? Why did the procession begin at the baptismal font? Why did we start with sprinkling everyone with water? Why do we call forth each candidate by name? What does it mean that someone stands with the candidate for this rite? Why at baptism are we anointed on the top of the head with words about belonging to Christ the Anointed One, while at confirmation we are anointed on the forehead with words about the Spirit? Why is this chrism oil so richly per-fumed? What does it mean that we lay hands on these people? There are dozens of such starting points in this liturgy, based as it is upon our ancient stories and gestures. This array of images, metaphors, stories and symbols waits to enliven the church's imagination again. They bid the homilist, in lieu of a vocations pitch to a captive audience, to announce the royal legacy and the call to service we share by our common baptism.

Chapter Six

Music

M usic unites the many individuals in the assembly
into a praying, celebrating community. By singing,
our words become prayer, our gathering becomes
animated, our many voices become one. Music engages
us in the symbolic actions, changes us from spectators and
recipients into participants and ministers. When the
musicians for the confirmation liturgy are involved in the
planning process, their knowledge and expertise help
reveal the spirit of the liturgy through its musical possibilities. Like the other planners, the musicians need to
become familiar with the rite itself and be attentive to the
proper and improper understandings of confirmation.

When to Sing

The Catholic liturgy is consistently a sung litany of praise
built around the musical dialogue between presider
and congregation and between cantor and congregation.
The primary musical elements of the Catholic liturgy
are not hymns; rather, the primary musical elements are
the sung acclamations and responses and the antiphonal
singing of the psalms. When preparing the confirmation liturgy or any other liturgy, first consideration is given
to the responsorial psalm, the gospel acclamation, the
acclamations of the eucharistic prayer, the litany during
the breaking of the bread, and the processional antiphon
during the sharing of the eucharist.

The confirmation ritual has its own musical require-
ments and possibilities. When the rite of sprinkling is used

in place of the penitential rite, an antiphon or appropriate song is sung by all. To affirm their own faith after the candidates have renewed their baptismal promises, the assembly joins in song (*Rite of Confirmation*, 23). The bishop preferably sings both the invitation to prayer and the prayer itself at the laying on of hands (#24–25). During the anointing with chrism, all may join in song (#29). The general intercessions, which follow the anointing (#30), easily lend themselves to a sung litany of prayer. If the prayer over the people is used for the blessing at the end of the liturgy (#33), it is preferable that it be sung.

The role of hymns is of secondary concern. The communion processional music is best done antiphonally, with the congregation repeating a refrain familiar enough to require no worship aid or hymnal. The use of a congregational hymn during the presentation of the gifts is discouraged so as not to overemphasize this minor moment. The recessional music can properly be instrumental music alone.

The point is this: Music planning for the confirmation liturgy does not consist of choosing three or four Spirit-themed hymns. The planning begins with developing both a good understanding of confirmation, and a good sense of the entire liturgy. It means recognizing the central and essential role the rite assigns to congregational singing. It requires spending time and energy on all the service music the liturgy requires: psalms, antiphons, acclamations and refrains. Then, and only then, is it time to think about where hymns might be appropriate and what hymns to consider.

Rite of Confirmation

The role of music during the rite of confirmation itself is to intensify and enhance key moments. We examine four points of the confirmation rite to suggest both possibilities and cautions about the music involved: the renewal of baptismal promises, the laying on of hands, the anointing with chrism and the general intercessions.

Renewal of Baptismal Promises

The candidates' profession of faith is confirmed by the bishop and the congregation (#40). The bishop may use the suggested formula ("This is our faith . . ."), or he may state this in his own words ("some other formula may be substituted"); to any such proclamation, the congregation adds its assent by responding "Amen." The rite suggests another way for the bishop and the whole assembly to affirm and acclaim this profession of faith: "The community may express its faith in a suitable song." This affirmation of faith is made stronger if it is sung — many voices becoming one voice, proclaiming one shared faith. This is not a good time for a lengthy hymn; it is an excellent time for a sung refrain or acclamation.

Laying on of Hands

The bishop calls the assembly to prayer (#41), then he alone proclaims the prayer of consecration: "Send your Holy

Spirit upon them to be their Helper and Guide" (#42). The rite suggests that both the invitation to prayer and the prayer of consecration may be sung by the bishop. If music serves to intensify the moment, it seems especially appropriate that the prayer of consecration be sung. This solemn invocation is the verbal expression of what the actions (laying on of hands and anointing) will make explicit. The fact that presidential prayers are not commonly sung would make the singing or chanting of this prayer all the more striking. In contrast, singing the call to prayer (#41) is of less importance and may detract from the prominence of the sung prayer of consecration.

Planners need to be careful about music during the laying on of hands, lest the primary actions of the rite get lost and overwhelmed. If the bishop and priests will only extend their hands over all for the prayer of consecration, invite the entire assembly to be part of this by joining in song after the bishop's call to prayer ("Let us pray to our Father that he will pour out the Holy Spirit . . ."). A short acclamation at this point (perhaps the sung "Lord, hear our prayer" usually used with the intercessions), before the imposition of hands and sung prayer of consecration, can help the action and solemn prayer become an expression of the prayer of all.

If the family groups will lay hands on the candidates while the ministers extend hands over all, it is best that this go on without singing or musical accompaniment. This action should be allowed to express this invocation of God's Spirit on its own. If instead the ministers will move toward the candidates, or the candidates process to the ministers for the laying on of hands, then this movement and imposition of hands could also be done in silence. Any music at this moment could easily detract from, rather than intensify, this strong gesture. The sung prayer of consecration would follow the imposition of hands.

Anointing

The anointing with chrism and the accompanying blessing of peace should likewise take place without singing by the assembly. There is the pouring out and presentation of the chrism to the other ministers by the bishop, the move-ment of people (ministers to the candidates or candidates with sponsors to the ministers), the actions of anointing and of placing hands on the candidates' shoulders, the words with the anointing (at which the candidate's name is used), and the blessing of peace. Let these actions themselves speak to the assembly; this is not a good time for busying everyone with singing. The exception may be when this anointing will take a long time because of a large number of candidates, even if additional ministers are involved. In this case, let the anointing go on awhile in silence, then use music as low-key background during the latter part of the procession. An organ and flute arrangement of the plainchant "Veni, Creator Spiritus," for example, may help to enhance and intensify the actions. If in doubt, avoid singing during this time.

General Intercessions

The rite of confirmation concludes with the general intercessions. Especially if there has been little music during
the rite of confirmation, singing the intercessions is a good
way to bring the rite to a close. The cantor leads everyone
in a litany of prayer, bringing the liturgy of the word and the
words and actions of the confirmation rite together in a
summary of sung petition.

Music Ministers

Much of the service music of the confirmation liturgy is
meant to be a musical dialogue of prayer between the cantor
(or other ministers) and the assembly: the antiphon with
the sprinkling rite, the responsorial psalm, the gospel acclamation, the general intercessions, the acclamations of

the eucharistic prayer, the litany for the breaking of the bread, the communion processional. The listening-and-responding pattern of these pieces reflects the fundamental pattern for all liturgical prayer. This requires that close attention be given to the many musical roles in the liturgy: cantor, congregation, instrumentalists, bishop, deacon, choir or schola. The cantor especially must be well-prepared to lead a practice with the assembly beforehand and to invite their song throughout the liturgy.

The congregation and its active participation are vital to the dynamics of the liturgy. A short and well-organized practice before the liturgy begins can prepare the assembly for its essential role and form the necessary rapport between the cantor and congregation. The practice is not only for the purpose of rehearsing the music, but also for coaxing and relaxing people enough to help them let go in song. The congregation at a confirmation liturgy is often so heterogeneous that the people need to hear themselves in practice if they are going to sing together well, even if they are already familiar with the music.

Selecting Music

Planners will want to avoid using lots of new or unfamiliar music for this liturgy. Because this gathering will probably include people from many parish communities, it is important to search for music familiar to as many people as possible. At the same time, the uniqueness of this occasion and of this assembly makes it a good opportunity to stretch everyone's musical and liturgical experience.

As mentioned before, the problem is not finding good and appropriate music for this liturgy; the problem will be narrowing down the many excellent offerings available. Go back to the suggested responsorial psalms for confirmation in the rite (#63), and investigate musical settings for these six psalms. The psalms and the antiphons listed can provide leads for the selection of the music for the gathering and sprinkling rites, the psalm itself, singing (if any) during the anointing with chrism, the communion processional, and possibly a recessional hymn. In addition, most liturgical music publishers have sections in their catalogs on music for Christian initiation. Consult your parish music collection and resource people as well.

Remember that we do not reinvent liturgy each time we come to it, nor do we create the music from scratch. This is a parish initiation liturgy, with everything in common with the parish's other initiation liturgies. Look at the common repertoire your parish already has for initiation, especially for the Easter Vigil. What Easter, initiatory or vigiling psalms, acclamations and sung prayers does the parish already know? What music does the parish use on the Sundays of Easter for the sprinkling rite? What acclamations are sung at the Easter Vigil as people are baptized or anointed, or as the assembly renews its baptismal vows? What musical settings of psalms are used for Easter Vigil or the Sundays of Easter? What acclamations are sung when your parish celebrates the baptism of infants? All this is part of the parish's musical repertoire for initiation, and this is the starting point for the music of this liturgy of initiation as well.

The planning process need not be as difficult as we sometimes make it. Instead, we ask the question that helps us situate this confirmation liturgy (and also its music) in the most appropriate context: What does this liturgy have in common with the other celebrations of initiation that occur in this parish community? The use of music will convey our theology of confirmation as boldly as any aspect of the liturgy can. This liturgy and its music should not outshine every other parish liturgy; this is a parish initiation liturgy, not an annual visit-of-the-bishop liturgy. This liturgy is not the only, or even the primary, celebration of the gift of Christ's Spirit; it is not appropriate simply to use "Come, Holy Ghost" or another Spirit-themed hymn just because it is familiar to people. Our practice and understanding of confirmation are changing; the music we use for confirmation must reflect that development. The other planners need the expertise of the musicians, but the musicians need the expertise of the liturgists and catechists as well, so that the music of the liturgy can reflect the larger context of initiation in which the church now places confirmation.

Chapter Seven

Places and People

At various times in the confirmation liturgy, people have to move from one place to another. The processions and the logistics of moving around call for careful planning so that everyone's involvement is enhanced. Otherwise, the situation can easily appear chaotic and participation in the liturgy can be adversely affected.

Processions

Think of the processions that are a standard part of our eucharistic liturgy: the entrance procession, the procession for the reading of the gospel, the preparation of the altar and procession with the gifts, and the communion procession. Each of these focuses our attention on what follows; they give a sense of movement and progression, of redirection and change.

The Entrance Procession

The entrance procession begins the liturgy, drawing us from our scattered and private thoughts to a common readiness for the word and the eucharist. Who and what is to be in this procession for the confirmation liturgy? The scriptures, the lector(s), the baptismal water, the Easter candle, the chrism, incense, the bishop, the deacon(s) and the concelebrating priests. The confirmation candidates, who then will be seated with the rest of the assembly, are certainly appropriate participants in this procession.

The Gospel Procession

This is a good occasion to emphasize the gospel by a procession of the book of the gospels (from the altar, where it has been enthroned, to the ambo) with candles and incense. If candles are used, who will carry them? Who will bring the thurible (incense pot or bowl) and the incense boat to the presider so that he can place incense on the coals?

The Procession with the Gifts

Since confirmation finds its culmination in the eucharist (*Rite of Confirmation*, 13), preparing the altar and the procession with the gifts both deserve to be highlighted at this liturgy. They can become a dressing-of-the-altar procession, which will draw the assembly to the table of the Lord for the climax of the entire celebration. Include the cloth for the altar, the one plate of bread and the decanter(s) of wine, then the candles and flowers to be placed near (but not on) the altar. Have those in the procession put all these items in their proper places. (One person can bring the sacramentary and one cup from the side table to the altar.) The last item in this procession can be the thurible, which is brought to the presider to put incense on the coals. After the gifts and the assembly are honored with incense, the thurible may be placed on the floor before the altar.

Some of the people in this procession should be the newly confirmed. In theory, if not in practice, this is their first celebration of the eucharist as fully initiated members of the church, and, like neophytes at the Easter Vigil, it is most appropriate for them to prepare the table of the Lord (RC, 31b). Such a dressing of the altar requires careful rehearsing and coordination to give it a measured and orderly pace. If done well, it can touch people deeply and evoke a clear sense of gathering everyone for the feast.

The Communion Procession

The communion procession is ideally the most joyful moment of the entire liturgy. The communion ministers, having prepared the bread and wine for distribution, move from the altar to their predetermined places. The assembly, joining in familiar and repetitive song with the cantor, comes forward to share in the eucharistic food. Communion from the cup is offered to all at this initiation liturgy, since initiation "reaches its culmination in the communion of the body and blood of Christ" (#13). Even if this is not a standard part of a parish's Sunday liturgies,

it should always be part of every parish initiation liturgy.
Arrange for sufficient communion ministers and vessels to
allow this sacred sharing to take place smoothly and in a
reasonably brief time. Generally, this requires two ministers
with cups for each minister with the consecrated bread.
If this is not the usual parish practice, this might require
some rehearsal with the ministers of communion.

Rite of Confirmation

The logistics for the rite of confirmation need careful
thought: Which people will need to move around? Where
will they be positioned? When will they move? The seating arrangements will affect how well people become involved
in the liturgy. In particular, the three moments in the
rite will require advance planning: the presentation of the
candidates, the laying on of hands, and the anointing.

Presentation of the Candidates

The candidates will stand to be presented to the bishop
after the readings. If possible, each is called by name and
presented individually; however, if there are too many to
present individually they may be presented as a group. The
rite indicates that the candidates move to the sanctuary
or some other suitable place before the bishop after being
presented (#21). However, not many church spaces allow
for all candidates to be comfortably accommodated in
the sanctuary during the homily. It would seem best that each
candidate stand in place when he or she is presented and
remain in place until all are presented, at which time all sit

down again for the homily. After the homily, the candidates alone stand for the renewal of baptismal promises (#23).

Laying on of Hands

If, as is preferable, the bishop and other ministers of confirmation lay hands upon each candidate (#9, 24, 25), arrange for the candidates to move forward for this and then return to their places. Or, in order to center this action in the midst of the assembly, arrange for the candidates to move into the aisles when they stand for the renewal of baptismal promises. Have them remain there, and have the ministers go to them for the laying on of hands (#26). Everyone else should remain seated so the laying on of hands is easily visible to all. This arrangement can help assure that the laying on of hands, which "is to be strongly emphasized for the integrity of the rite and the fuller understanding of the sacrament" (#9), is made as accessible as possible to everyone.

There is a third possible arrangement for the imposition of hands. A large number of candidates is an added reason for the bishop to include other priests as fellow ministers in this sacrament. But if the setting does not allow for the ministers to lay hands on the individual candidates, then have at least the sponsor, if not parents and other family members, impose hands as the ministers extend their hands over all. This has the advantage of requiring less movement than the individual imposition of hands, while at the same time engaging the assembly in the sacred action.

The candidates might move into the aisle for the renewal of baptismal promises; then the sponsor (and others) join them at the bishop's call to prayer and impose hands during the time of prayer.

Anointing

As with the laying on of hands, the candidates may go to the bishop and priests, or the ministers may go to the candidates (#26, 28). The simpler arrangement would be for the ministers to remain stationary and the candidates, accompanied by sponsors, to move forward to a minister for the anointing. The more significant arrangement would be for the candidates to stand in the aisles, in the midst of the assembly, and for the anointing to take place throughout the worship space. The bishop need not be seated nor the candidates kneeling for the anointing; the rite does not mention this at all.

Remember the priorities in planning: the symbolic actions visible and accessible to all, the entire assembly as engaged in them as possible. Don't limit your planning simply to what has been done in past years. Symbols that are made neat, tidy and efficient are not necessarily as effective, evocative and engaging as they are meant to be. The sanctuary area is not the only place for these symbols and actions; there are alternatives. Explore various possibilities before settling on what seems best for your situation.

In the same way, think about those who accompany the candidates for the anointing. The confirmation sponsor stands with the candidate for the anointing, placing a hand on the candidate's shoulder. The sponsor represents the whole church presenting the candidate for confirmation, expressing the commitment of the church to support and stand by this person. But it is certainly appropriate to invite the whole family to do the same: to express the commitment of the church to the candidate by standing next to him or her and placing a hand on the person's shoulder. Especially in small parish settings it is easy to arrange for parents to join sponsors during the anointing. This option requires the movement of more people than just candidate and sponsor, and therefore careful planning, but even large parishes and large congregations can work around these considerations. The effect of the family participating in the anointing itself can be very beneficial to the liturgy (further engaging the entire assembly in the sacramental actions) and to the understanding of confirmation itself.

Including Catechumens

It makes good sense for the parish's catechumens and candidates for full communion to be included in confirmation liturgies at which the bishop is presiding. These catechumens and candidates would take part in the liturgy of the word in the usual way. As a group they are presented to the bishop just before the confirmation candidates are presented. Ideally, their sponsors would be present to stand alongside them. The bishop would then greet them with words of support and encouragement and lay hands on them in prayer and blessing. The bishop would also commend them to the parish for continued guidance. The catechumens and candidates would then be dismissed in the usual way, and the rite of confirmation would proceed.

There are several good reasons for including the catechumens and candidates in this liturgy. First, their contact with the bishop, who is the chief pastor of the diocese and is responsible for their initiation into the church, is usually very limited. It is certainly appropriate for him to greet them and pray over them while he is presiding at this initiation liturgy in the parish. Second, confirmation itself is a sacramental celebration of prayer, support and encouragement along the journey of faith; highlighting the catechumens and candidates or the neophytes helps place confirmation in this larger parish picture and emphasizes the initiatory nature of confirmation. Further, including the catechumens and candidates helps express the unity and centrality of initiation in the parish.

Making arrangements for the catechumens and candidates and their sponsors at this liturgy places extra demands upon the planners, but is well worth the effort.

Seating
Should the confirmation candidates and the sponsors be seated separately from the rest of the congregation? This may

be the most efficient arrangement, but not necessarily the best one. If all the symbolic actions will be confined to the sanctuary area, if the ministers will simply extend their hands over all candidates, if the candidates and sponsors will go to the ministers for the anointing, if the families will not be involved in the actions, then this segregated seating will work efficiently. But if the symbols and actions will be brought into the assembly, if the assembly will be directly involved in these actions, if the ministers will be going to the candidates for the laying on of hands and/or the anointing, it would be far better for the candidates and sponsors to be seated with families and friends.

In any case, seating candidates and sponsors among the rest of the assembly has two advantages. First, it stresses that the family, a small model of the church itself, is the primary community responsible for presenting this person for confirmation. The parents "will be the first teachers of their child in the ways of faith. May they be also the best of teachers" (*Rite of Baptism for Children*, 105). It helps prevent a "graduation" approach to confirmation, and instead situates it as a continuation of baptism, when the parents, family and community gave ritual expression to their duty of sharing their faith with the child. Second, seating the candidates and sponsors with the rest of the assembly can enhance participation in the entire liturgy. The liturgical customs of the parish and the music used in this liturgy will be most familiar to the members of the parish, the candidates and family members. Seating sponsors,

visiting relatives and friends with the parish members will
affect how welcome and comfortable people are made to feel,
which will affect how well they participate.

The Site

With various options in mind, and realizing what this liturgy
can be, we need to consider the possibility of an alternative
site for confirmation. The problem is apparent: In so
many ways we are prisoners of our church buildings. We and
our liturgies must conform to our worship space, which so
often limits our liturgical practice. People are not able to
understand confirmation in a renewed way because they are
not able to experience it in a renewed way. We don't see
new dimensions of confirmation because our buildings do
not allow us to have new experiences of it. The document
Environment and Art in Catholic Worship (United States Bishops'
Committee on the Liturgy, 1978) makes it clear that
our worship space is to conform to our liturgical needs
and options, not the other way around.

Can we consider celebrating confirmation somewhere
that allows the seating and space and possible arrangements
to be flexible and adaptable? The chair, ambo and altar
do not have to be bunched together. The sanctuary area is not
the one holy place in our church building. The symbolic
actions are not meant to be confined to one small area
of our worship space. Moving people around frequently and
easily for this liturgy and engaging the assembly in the

actions are important priorities, but are difficult to achieve when the liturgy takes place in a restrictive space.

Think of the possibilities for arranging the space and processions to express an obvious change of focus at various points in the liturgy. The chair and ambo and altar would each have its own prominent spot; the grouping of the initiation elements (water, Easter candle, chrism) would likewise be a prominent focal point. The laying on of hands would become an arrangement of "prayer clusters" throughout the assembly, involving many if not all the people. As the bishop and priests extend hands and pray over all, everyone else would gather around each of the candidates, laying on hands and praying for them. The anointing might mean each family group presenting and accompanying and standing with the sponsor and candidate as the ministers move out to them from the bishop's chair. In this setting, the whole church is the minister of confirmation. The bishop becomes the presider over a gathering of ministers, and the assembly is not just witnessing the sacred actions but is part of them.

Is there a school gym or an open assembly hall that can be used for this confirmation liturgy? On the next few pages are some possible arrangements for such a space, whether there are movable chairs for seating or bleachers. Remember the priorities and liturgical goals. Explore the possibilities in the planning process; think about how best to arrange this liturgy for your own situation.

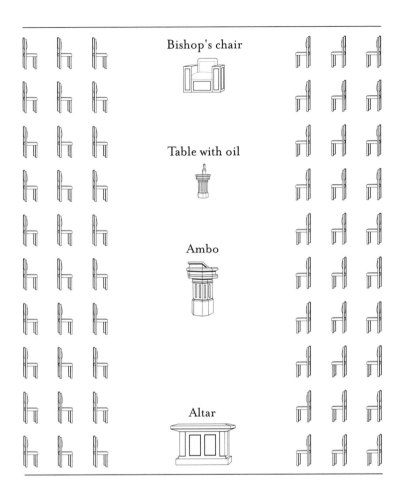

Figure 1. This arrangement encourages a change of focus during the liturgy from one end of the space to the other: from the bishop's chair to the ambo to the altar. The processions — entrance, gospel, confirmation rite, preparation of the altar and communion — become movements that shift our attention from one place to another as the ritual progresses. The bishop may well remain at the chair until processing to the altar for the eucharist. The imposition of hands and anointing could be presided over by the bishop from the chair, with these actions taking place all around the central area. This arrangement allows for the easy movement of many people for the confirmation rite.

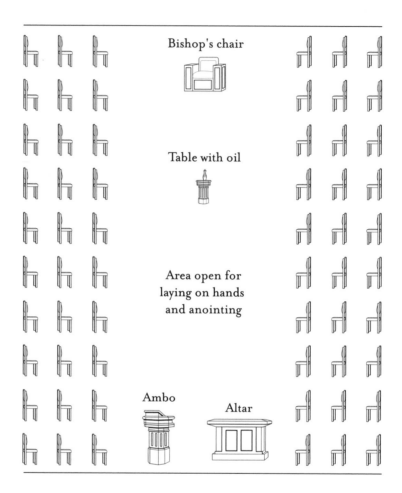

Bishop's chair

Table with oil

Area open for
laying on hands
and anointing

Ambo

Altar

Figure 2. This variation may be especially useful if the candidates will move toward the ministers for the laying on of hands and/or anointing. The ministers could move from the bishop's chair to their places in the open area, and remain there while the candidates (with sponsors and/or family groups) process to them.

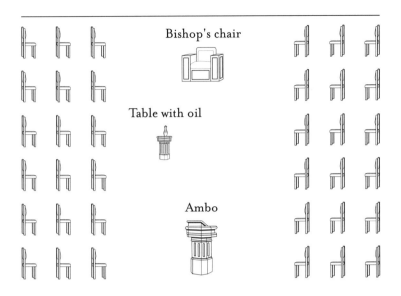

Bishop's chair

Table with oil

Ambo

Altar

Figure 3. In each of the first two diagrams, the dressing-of-the-altar procession becomes a procession of both the gifts and of the presider. In figure 3, the entire assembly could move to the far end of the area for the liturgy of the eucharist. This arrangement is feasible especially with a small assembly, when the entire space available would not be needed for seating and the confirmation rite. In this setting, the preparation of the altar becomes a procession of everyone to surround the table of the Lord for the sacred meal, which is the culmination of the initiation process.

Chapter Eight
The Ministers

The Assembly

It is the responsibility of the people of God
to prepare the baptized for confirmation.
(*Rite of Confirmation*, 3)

The whole people of God, represented by the families
and friends of the candidates and by the members of
the local community, will be invited to take part in
the celebration and will express its faith in the fruits
of the Holy Spirit. (RC, 4)

Revision of the church's rites during the last generation
has encompassed more than the streamlining of actions
and the rewriting of texts. The revision, with varying degrees
of success, has attempted to provide new images of our life
and relationships as the church. We are still trying to grow
into some of these new images.

The rites consistently insist that we exist as church
to proclaim faith and to foster faith in others. Our most
central task as church is to share with others faith in
Jesus Christ. The first and foremost minister of initiation
is the church itself.

The church believes it is its most basic and necessary
duty to inspire all, catechumens, parents of children still to be baptized, and godparents, to that true
and living faith by which they adhere to Christ and

enter into or confirm their commitment to the
new covenant. (General Introduction to *Christian
Initiation* [GI], 3)

The preparation for baptism and Christian instruction are both of vital concern to God's people,
the Church, which hands on and nourishes the faith
received from the apostles. Through the ministry
of the church, adults are called to the gospel by the
Holy Spirit and infants are baptized in the faith
of the church and brought up in that faith. (GI, 7)

Again and again in the rites of initiation, the first
minister to be listed is the church itself: "God's people, the
Church" (GI, 7); "the people of God, as represented by
the local Church" (*Rite of Christian Initiation of Adults* [RCIA],
9); "the People of God, that is the Church" (*Rite of Baptism
for Children* [RBC], 4).

The people of God . . . should understand and
show by their concern that the initiation of
adults is the responsibility of all the baptized. The
community must always be fully prepared in the
pursuit of its apostolic vocation to give help to those
who are searching for Christ. . . . All the followers of Christ have the obligation of spreading
the faith according to their abilities. Hence,
the entire community must help the candidates and

catechumens throughout the process of initiation.
(RCIA, 9; emphasis added)

The intention is certainly clear: Initiation is the
responsibility of all the baptized. Initiation belongs to the
church and is the reason for which the church exists. The
same image is reflected in the *Rite of Confirmation:* "It is
the responsibility of the people of God to prepare the baptized for confirmation" (#3).

The ministry of initiating people into the living body
of Christ is not the monopoly of anyone in the church. The
primary minister of initiation is the community, the people called together by the Lord, chosen to be the dwelling
place of the Spirit. The parish assembly as a whole bears the
responsibility for presenting the candidates for confirmation; it expresses the assembly's very reason for existence.

Confirmation, like all the other sacraments, has as
much to do with the growth of the entire community as with
the growth of the individual candidate. The confirming of
the candidates becomes the occasion, the focus around which
the entire assembly renews its faith and is itself confirmed
as the body of Christ. "Sacraments happen not to the individual but to the assembly of the Lord's people" (Tad
Guzie, *The Book of Sacramental Basics,* New York: Paulist Press,
1981, page 60). It is not the candidates being sealed or
affirmed by this liturgy. Rather, what is sealed is the baptismal gift of the Spirit, and that gift of the Spirit is always

a communal one. We celebrate confirmation because of the assembly's life in the Spirit; we mark candidates with the chrism because there is a Spirit-filled community, and so that there will always be a Spirit-filled community. In sharing our life in Christ's Spirit with the candidates, in celebrating the gift of the Spirit with them, the entire parish community is renewed in that baptismal way of life.

The liturgical expression of confirmation or of any sacrament is a display of the real and envisioned life of the community of faith, of church, not solely or simply of the individual. Whether the sacrament works for an individual is not the issue. Rather, the crucial question is whether or not the sacramental action expresses the life of the community and challenges it as well. (See Stephen Happel's "Speaking from Experience: Worship and the Social Sciences," in *Alternative Futures for Worship, Vol. 2: Baptism and*

Confirmation, ed. Mark Searle, Collegeville: Liturgical Press, 1987, pages 171–184.)

In preparing the candidates, the parish assembly is itself called to examine its life and spirit, called to grow and to be renewed. Is it presumptuous of us to celebrate the presence of the Spirit in our midst? Does our common life in fact bear witness to the Spirit of Christ? Are we asking the candidates to pledge themselves to something we as a community do not honestly believe in and live? "The local community will express its faith in the fruits of the Holy Spirit" (RC, 4). How then do we help the whole parish own this celebration? Certainly this needs attention long before the liturgical celebration.

There should be clear indications that the parish gives special attention to those whom we initiate into the church: parents and families preparing for the baptism of children, catechumens and candidates for full communion, those preparing for first eucharist, and those preparing for confirmation. Remembering them and their families in the general intercessions draws attention and concern to them. Having older members of the parish (including parishioners confined to their homes or nursing homes) adopt one of the candidates as a prayer partner, and making sure the candidate has contact with his or her prayer partner, can do wonders for the candidate and for the older parishioner.

The candidate has valuable contact with a much more sea-
soned person of faith and prayer, and the older parishioner
discovers there is a vital role in the life of the parish for
the infirm and aged. Through a Christian service project,
the candidate can be of service to the parish or community,
getting into the practice of ministering to the needs of
others. In these ways the parish at large is directly involved
in preparing candidates for confirmation.

Certainly the parish is to be made aware of the confirmation liturgy and invited to take part, for it is our
communal life that is being celebrated. Are there so many
candidates that attendance has to be restricted to sponsors and family members? One alternative would be to plan
confirmation liturgies more frequently — every year
instead of every other, or twice in one year instead of one
crowded celebration. The sense should be that the parish
is hosting this liturgy, not that parishioners are tolerated
at the celebration if there are empty seats. The goal is that
visitors join with the parish assembly for this liturgy,
not that the visitors make up the vast majority of the congregation. Visitors will nevertheless be numerous for this
special occasion, and they need to be welcomed.

Parishioners ministering as greeters for the liturgy can
help to seat people and to ensure an atmosphere of hospitality for all visitors. In addition, other parishioners can
be called upon to serve in the other liturgical ministries
this celebration requires.

Parents

> The initiation of children into the sacramental
> life is for the most part the responsibility and
> concern of Christian parents. They are to form
> and gradually increase a spirit of faith in the
> children and . . . prepare them for the fruitful
> reception of . . . confirmation and the eucha-
> rist. The role of parents is also expressed by their
> active participation in the celebration of the
> sacraments. (RC, 3)

By asking for baptism, parents accept the responsibility
of training the child in the practice of the faith, of bringing
them into the sacramental life of the church. This solemn
duty is not the parents' task alone; the whole community,
along with its priests and catechists, is responsible for
surrounding the parents with help, encouragement, support
and living examples of faith in the Lord. Still, the primary
community of faith in the church is the family. While
catechesis articulates our faith and the parish community
celebrates our faith, it rests with the household to enflesh
the way of life into which baptism calls us.

Confirmation has to do not only with the candidates but
with the whole assembly. The preparation challenges the
candidates to examine their lives of faith, and it also calls
the parish, parents and households to conversion and
new growth. Do we live as disciples of Christ? Is the Spirit

of Christ apparent in our lives and actions, in our midst?
Are our children pledging themselves to something we
as adults do not believe in and live? Parents are to "prepare
them for the fruitful reception . . . of confirmation and
the eucharist." And "by their active participation in the
celebration of the sacraments," parents further express their
role as the first and best of teachers.

The nature of ritual is that it celebrates and makes
explicit what has been going on long before the ritual itself
takes place. The confirmation liturgy is a sealing of the life
in Christ's Spirit, which the whole church, including the
candidates, is to be living already, a celebration of the faith
that is already present and apparent. This or any liturgy
is a summing up of the prayers and encounters with God
that have gone on in our lives already. As part of the living
example of discipleship, parents are to be people of prayer,
praying as a family, praying with the child who is a candidate for confirmation. Part of that example is to show that
praying with the whole community of faith by "active participation in the celebration of the sacraments" is essential.
The active participation of the parents and families in
this confirmation liturgy is dependent upon the quality
of prayer and active participation within the home
and the parish. The ministry of the parents in this liturgy
really takes place long before the liturgy itself. The task
for the planners is to make this liturgy an authentic expression, a communal summing up, of what has been going on
in hearts and homes already.

Sponsors

It is helpful to read paragraph five of the Introduction to
the *Rite of Confirmation:*

> Ordinarily there should be a sponsor for each of
> those to be confirmed. The sponsor brings the
> candidate to receive the sacrament, presents him to
> the minister for the anointing and will later help
> him to fulfill his baptismal promises faithfully under
> the influence of the Holy Spirit.
>
> In view of contemporary pastoral circumstances,
> it is desirable that the godparent at baptism, if
> present, also be the sponsor at confirmation. . . .
> This . . . expresses more clearly the relationship
> between baptism and confirmation and also makes
> the function and responsibility of the sponsor
> more effective.
>
> Nonetheless the choice of a special sponsor for
> confirmation is not excluded. Even the parents them-
> selves may present their children for confirmation.
> It is for the local ordinary to determine diocesan
> practice after considering local circumstances.

The rite continues the ancient baptismal practice of
each candidate having a sponsor (as with each catechumen
or each infant to be baptized). Note that there is no
requirement for the sponsor to be of the same sex as the
candidate. The rite assumes that the sponsor is chosen

by the candidate or family (RC, 6). Pastors are charged
to make sure sponsors are "spiritually qualified for the
office." They are to be sufficiently mature, be members
of the church, and be fully initiated by baptism, confirmation, and eucharist. The ministry of the sponsor is
primarily in the future, to "later help [the candidate] to
fulfill his [or her] baptismal promises faithfully" (#5).
The rite envisions a close, continuing bond of faith shared
and nourished, meant as more than a mere formality.

The person is to be "spiritually qualified," someone who
can give that essential, living example of faith, someone
who gives evidence of fulfilling his or her "baptismal promises
faithfully under the influence of the Holy Spirit." What is
the significance of the sponsor? For a catechumen, the
sponsor is an adult member of the church who is a prayer
companion during the catechumenate, who offers support
and encouragement, who serves as the personal representative of the parish for the catechumen and is a sign of
the community's commitment to this new member. Often
this same person then is asked by the catechumen to be
a godparent, the companion during the final preparation
for the sacraments and the extended mystagogia that follows. The role of the godparent at infant baptism is
derived from this catechumenal role, but it has more to
do with the parents than it does with the infant: "Are you
ready to help these parents in their duty as Christian
mothers and fathers?" (RBC, 40) Here the baptismal

godparent is intended as companion more to the parents than to the infant.

From this background, the *Rite of Confirmation* (#5) urges that the baptismal godparent be the confirmation sponsor, to "express more clearly the relationship between baptism and confirmation" and to make "the function and responsibility of the sponsor more effective." Especially if we assume a short time span between infant baptism and confirmation (which the rite does) then the suggestion of the baptismal godparent moving from a relationship with the parents to a relationship with the child makes sense. As a second choice, the rite permits a "special sponsor" for confirmation, but this is clearly a second choice, one which the rite tolerates but does not encourage. If we are to be consistent in reemphasizing confirmation's relation to baptism, then the practice of choosing a special confirmation sponsor should be discouraged.

The *Code of Canon Law* repeats the rite's insistence on this baptismal connection. The sponsor seeks to assure "that the confirmed person acts as a true witness to Christ and faithfully fulfills the obligations connected with this sacrament" (canon 892). "It is desirable that the one who undertook the role of sponsor at baptism be sponsor for confirmation" (canon 893; see also canon 874). Though the *Rite of Confirmation* even made room for parents to be sponsors, canon law, which was revised after the rite was promulgated, reiterated the baptismal character of this

ministry, clearly paralleling it to the sponsor and godparent
with catechumens and neophytes or to the godparent for
an infant who is baptized. In all these initiatory situations,
the sponsors are a reminder that these people are initiated
into a community of faith greater than the household,
a reminder that the wider church has a role and a stake in
this initiation. The parents and family have a central role
in initiation which is supplemented by other members
of the church. Sponsors manifest that wider circle of faith
into which the candidates are initiated, which leads the
revised code to urge that the confirmation sponsor be
the baptismal sponsor and definitely someone other than
the candidate's parent.

Bishop and Priests

The bishop is the chief pastor of the diocese, "the leader
of the entire liturgical life in the church committed to them"
(GI, 12). It is for the bishop, "in person or through his
delegate, to set up, regulate and promote the pastoral formation of catechumens" (RCIA, 44). While bishops, priests
and deacons are the "ordinary ministers of baptism" (GI, 11),
the bishop is the primary minister [minister originarius] of
confirmation" (RC, 7).

What does this mean? It means that the bishop is the
one responsible for the practices of Christian initiation and
the celebration of the sacraments of initiation in the diocese, that priests and deacons assist and cooperate with the
bishop and serve in their roles as delegated by the bishop.

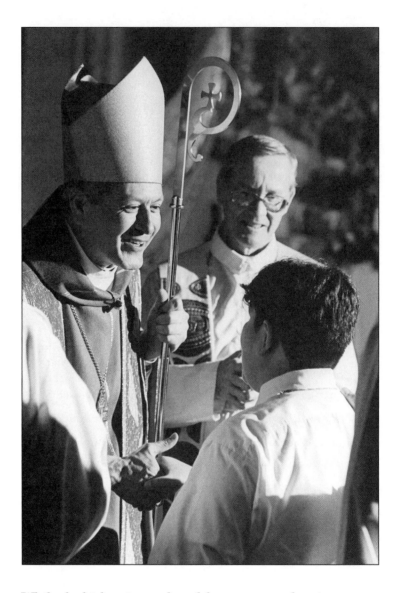

While the bishop is not the celebrant at every baptism,
the celebrant is in fact the bishop's representative and local
delegate. We are accustomed to priests and deacons being
the ministers at baptism; we are not accustomed to priests
being the usual ministers of confirmation. But in fact

the priest is the normal minister of confirmation for any adults or children of catechetical age who are baptized or received into full communion. The priest presiding at the Easter Vigil, for example, is to make sure that those elect who are baptized and those candidates who are received into full communion are confirmed as part of that same liturgy. "Adult catechumens . . . are to be confirmed immediately after baptism" (RC, 3). At the Easter Vigil, the presider not only may confirm these people but must confirm them. In other words, the physical presence of the bishop is not essential to the celebration of confirmation, and the bishop is not its only minister.

The *Rite of Confirmation* itself makes clear that the bishop can "associate other priests with himself in the administration of this sacrament" when, for example, there is a large number of candidates (#8). These may be priests with a particular function or office in the diocese, the candidates' pastors, or priests with a special role in the candidates' catechesis. In some dioceses, confirmation is celebrated at the regional or even diocesan level, rather than in a single parish. These large liturgies, when there may be several hundred candidates for confirmation, take place only because many presbyters join with the bishop as ministers for the imposition of hands and anointing. In a growing number of dioceses within the United States and elsewhere, the traditional order of the sacraments of initiation has been restored, so that confirmation is celebrated before or along with the candidates' first reception of communion.

In these dioceses, the pastor and other presbyters become
the normal ministers of confirmation (parallel to the experience of the Easter Vigil liturgy). The code of canon law
provides for the local bishop to delegate certain priests of his
diocese as ministers of confirmation in his place: "If necessity requires it, the diocesan bishop can grant the faculty
to one or several priests to administer this sacrament." (See
canon 838.1. Before the current revision of canon law, such
permission could only be granted by special indult from
Rome.) While it may be a new experience for a particular
parish to see priests imposing hands and anointing at a
confirmation liturgy along with the bishop, this practice
is hardly new or drastic.

The balance between confirmation as initiation by the
church and as a liturgy with the bishop is not a new question
in Roman Catholic circles. The revision of the rite of
confirmation is described by Archbishop Annibale Bugnini,
a key figure in the process. His description includes
discussions of most of our questions and dilemmas about
confirmation (*The Reform of the Liturgy, 1948–1975*,
Collegeville: The Liturgical Press, 1990). The "long and
wearisome" revision process struggled to clarify the question
of the proper minister of the sacrament. Pope Paul VI
raised objections to any diminishment of the place of the
bishop in the rite: "For, once the new rite allows bishops
to use the help of simple [*sic*] priests even in the rite of
anointing with chrism, doubts and uncertainties may arise"

(Bugnini, pages 618–19 and footnote 16). Eventually, notes Bugnini,

> The new rite as a whole highlight[ed] the person
> of the bishop and contact with him as successor of the
> apostles and primary minister of this sacrament.
> See especially the homily, the end of the general inter-
> cessions, and the mention to be made of the bishop
> when the minister is not himself a bishop (RC, 18).
> Likewise, when the bishop decides to let priests
> play a role in the celebration . . . they receive the holy
> chrism from his hands to indicate that he is the
> primary minister and they his assistants. (page 620)

So the rite itself is inconsistent, calling the church the primary minister of initiation but reluctant to accept some of the challenges, changes and consequences this revised ecclesiology implies.

The rite promotes confirmation as an initiation lit-urgy; our tradition promotes it as an episcopal liturgy. It is little wonder that our pastoral practice remains divided on this issue. In some dioceses, confirmation has now become a cathedral or diocesan liturgy for a variety of rea-sons including: a shortage of bishops in large archdioceses; episcopal schedules that cannot handle all the demands for confirmation liturgies; or the desire for a bigger, more public expression of Roman Catholic identity. These big liturgical events enjoy the support of some bishops, but it is difficult to find as much enthusiasm among the pastoral ministers, catechists, and families. While a public, even striking, display of diocesan identity may result, much is sacrificed for these episcopal liturgies. Here even the candidates, families and sponsors become visitors. Confirmation becomes grafted to the person of the bishop more than ever and is further diminished as an initiation liturgy of the local parish community. In addition, this "mega-confirmation" so inflates the sacrament that it further distorts its meaning, its proper place in the process of initiation, and the ecclesial context in which it belongs, aspects of confirmation that the revised rite intended to renew and reform.

Such large liturgies enhance the place of the bishop in confirmation, but this is hardly the minister whose place in confirmation needs enhancement, nor was enhancing the presider the intent of the reformed rite. The revised rite of confirmation called for a rethinking of our practice and theology of confirmation, but our pastoral practice indicates we still have a way to go. While the bishop remains the original minister of confirmation, we will continue more and more to see priests presiding at this liturgy as delegates of the bishop.

As noted earlier, part of the unfortunate pressure on confirmation liturgies at present is that they are often the only times the bishop is in the parish. Would it not be more authentic for the local pastor or regional vicar to preside at this initiation liturgy and to invite the bishop at some other time in the year to celebrate the eucharist? Special guests at that eucharist with the bishop could be all the parishioners involved in initiation in that year: parents whose children have been baptized, the neophytes of the parish, those who have celebrated first communion, and those confirmed. Then the bishop would be seen as directly involved with the whole of initiation in the parish, not just one aspect of it. After all, eucharist is the culmination of Christian initiation, not confirmation.

Pastors are charged "to see that all the baptized come to the fullness of Christian initiation and are carefully prepared for confirmation" (RC, 3), and that the sponsors are spiritually qualified for the office (#6). In other words, much of the priest's role is to support and work with the confirmation team of the parish: candidates and parents, sponsors, catechists, liturgists and musicians. Their ministry is to encourage and support others in their own ministries. The parish priests, more than anyone else, can set the tone and form the environment for confirmation, helping everyone involved to grow in the life of Christian faith.

Other Ministers

Planners will need to coordinate the other ministers for the liturgy: greeters, acolytes, lectors, eucharistic ministers, cantor and musicians. It may be very helpful, in addition, to have a master of ceremonies for this liturgy, since confirmation is celebrated so infrequently and involves much movement and action.

The greeters can help set the tenor of the liturgy by their gracious hospitality. They can welcome people, distribute booklets or songbooks, and help people be seated. Be sure they know the seating arrangements in advance and are conscious of making visitors feel welcome.

Acolytes will be busy with many details. This is a good occasion to have adults — women and men — serve as acolytes, rather than relying on younger members to keep everything straight. There will be extra objects, actions, movements and processions for the acolytes to attend to. Besides the sacramentary, there will be the ritual book for the rite of confirmation and the bishop's miter and crosier. In addition, a container for the chrism and a small towel will be needed for each minister who assists with the anointing. The chrism is brought to the bishop, along with the small containers and small towels. (If the bishop does not pour the chrism into the small containers, be clear about who will.) The bishop distributes the containers of chrism to each of the ministers for the anointing. Afterwards, one or more bowls of warm, soapy water and towels will be required at the credence table to wash the oil from the ministers' hands. Acolytes will need a clear idea of the entire liturgy and its special demands, and know when and where to be present. Rehearsal with them is a necessity.

It is preferable that the lectors be seated with the rest of the assembly until coming forward to proclaim the readings. In the same way, eucharistic ministers come forth from the assembly to help with the breaking of bread and the pouring out of wine, then move to their positions for the sharing of communion. Be sure there are enough communion ministers for sharing both the bread and the wine. The value of rehearsal with and coordination of all these ministers cannot be emphasized enough.

Rehearsal with candidates and sponsors is also very helpful. This liturgy is an infrequent occurrence in the parish community, often with a large congregation that includes many visitors. All the ministers must know what they are doing, when and where to move.

The cantor can help direct people's attention and involvement by word and gesture throughout the liturgy. At two points it may be helpful for someone to give an additional word of explanation. In the rite of confirmation itself, it will be helpful to explain how the laying on of hands will be done and what is expected of everyone. Then, as the communion procession is about to begin, a word of invitation for everyone to receive from the cup may be necessary (though reception from the cup is more common now). All other words of commentary and explanation are best left to a printed order of worship. Providing people with a brief sketch of the liturgy and its actions in printed form is helpful; providing a running commentary is excessive. Let the actions and the people's involvement in the celebration speak on their own.

Chapter Nine

Review for Planners

The planning process for the confirmation liturgy calls for background reading, homework, prayer and reflection, sharing, consistency, coordination of many ministers and evaluation of the liturgy afterward. What may appear to be overwhelming need not be.

Still, it is important for the planners to

* keep the proper perspectives on confirmation firmly in mind — what confirmation is and what it is not

* remember the initiatory context and elements of this liturgy

* consider the many people besides the candidates who have essential roles in this liturgy

* have an appreciation of the liturgy as a whole, while planning the separate parts of it

* start the preparation process early and evaluate the process afterward

* realize that the time and effort involved in planning are important gifts to the community, gifts which will be blessed and multiplied for the sake of all

We will take a brief look at the entire liturgy, making some final points and reviewing aspects that need attention. This is meant to help both in preparation and in evaluation. Make note of what goes well with this liturgy to avoid starting from scratch next time. Also make note of what should have been handled differently.

Advance Planning

Advance planning includes

* ensuring, well in advance, that the entire parish is involved in and made aware of confirmation, and is encouraged to take part in the liturgy

* deciding how to include the catechumens and candidates for full communion in the liturgy

* exploring alternative locations for the liturgy to facilitate involvement and to enhance the symbols

* preparing the liturgy of the word (readings and music) as a result of reflecting on the suggested scripture passages

* sharing the insights of this reflection process with the homilist

* acquiring enough chrism for it and its container to be significant and substantial; also acquiring an oil-based perfume to mix with the oil, if needed

* printing a simple booklet or order of worship with a bare outline of the liturgy, instructions or directions for the assembly, and music references or the music itself (be sure to obtain appropriate copyright permissions)

* rehearsing with all the liturgical ministers: greeters, lectors, cantor, acolytes, those in the entrance procession, ministers of the eucharist

* contacting a professional photographer to take photos or videos for everyone to avoid the distractions of many cameras and many flashes

Hospitality and Participation
Hospitality and participation require that

* candidates, sponsors, guests and family members are (preferably) all seated together, and seating arrangements are made for the priests who will minister the sacrament with the bishop

all who need to move during the liturgy (lectors, ministers of communion, candidates and
sponsors, etc.) have easy access to the aisles

* the greeters understand their responsibilities,
  know the seating arrangements, and arrive
  early to welcome and seat people and to
  distribute the booklet or order of worship

* planners adjust the site or arrangements
  to help all hear and see easily in order to
  participate well

* the assembly be reminded (by notes in a booklet or by simple instructions from a master
  of ceremonies) when only the candidates stand,
  when candidates and others move for the
  laying on of hands and anointing, when the
  entire assembly sits or stands

* planners arrange carefully for the presentation
  of the candidates, laying on of hands and the
  anointing

* the candidates and those standing with them
  understand how the laying on of hands and
  the anointing will proceed

* the cantor rehearses with the assembly and
  invites people to participate fully through
  the music

* a parish group sponsor a reception for
  everyone after the liturgy

Entrance Procession and Introductory Rites

Plans for the entrance procession and introductory
rites involve

* arranging for people to lead the procession
  with the water, oil, Easter candle (if it is
  of manageable size), gospel book (if a deacon

is participating) and thurible; then explaining
where these elements are to be placed

* deciding if the candidates will be a part of the
  entrance procession

* selecting a strong processional hymn

* using the sprinkling rite in place of the penitential rite (even if this liturgy takes place
  during Lent), knowing who will sprinkle the
  people (the bishop or a delegated minister)
  and how the minister will move among
  the assembly, and choosing an appropriate
  antiphon or acclamation for the sprinkling

* remembering that the Gloria, more appropriate to the Christmas and Easter seasons, is
  not obligatory for this liturgy, that if used it
  should be sung, and that it might be used
  as entrance music or as a post-communion
  piece for congregation and cantor

The Liturgy of the Word

The liturgy of the word is the cornerstone of the entire
liturgy. Remember its essential proclamation-and-response
rhythm, the importance of music during this word service,
how vital good and well-rehearsed lectors are. Remember,

too, that all our preparations for this liturgy begin by preparing the liturgy of the word. Specifically, this involves

* the gospel book carried in by the deacon and enthroned on the altar (if the gospel will not be proclaimed by a deacon, then the gospel book is enthroned on the altar before the liturgy begins)

* the cantor leading the responsorial psalm

* allowing for a time of silent reflection before and after the readings

* a procession of the gospel book, with sung acclamation, perhaps with candles and incense

* someone other than the bishop proclaiming the gospel (a deacon, or in his absence, one of the priests)

* sharing the results of the planners' and confirmation candidates' prayer and reflection about the liturgy and the scriptures with the homilist in advance

Rite of Confirmation

The rite is the most demanding part of the entire liturgy, involving many people and much movement and activity.

Think it through ahead of time, remembering that our
symbolic actions are to be visible and accessible to all, and
that we want the assembly fully engaged in them. Arrange
everything with these considerations in mind; be more
concerned with these than with being orderly and tidy.

The decisions concerning the location of the liturgy, the
number of ministers for the anointing, who serves as sponsors, the role of the catechumens in the liturgy, the laying
on of hands, ministers moving to the candidates or candidates
to the ministers, family groups standing with the candidates, and seating arrangements are all interrelated. These
decisions will be affected by the number of candidates
and by other particulars of your situation. But our perspec-
tive on confirmation, our liturgical principles and our
desire that this celebration engage those participating must
also affect these decisions.

While giving attention to each of its parts, keep the
rite as an integrated whole firmly in mind: a community,
anointed with the Spirit of Christ by baptism, shares
the scriptures to realize again its great dignity. Having done
so, the community calls forward and instructs younger
members, moving them to turn from evil toward faith.
By the ancient gestures of laying on hands and anointing,
the church marks these younger members as belonging
to the Anointed One and to his living body.

The whole assembly then celebrates the eucharist, the ultimate expression of oneness in the Lord.

Presentation of the Candidates

* Begin with the presentation of the catechumens and candidates for full communion (or neophytes and newly received members, if, ideally, confirmation takes place in the Easter season).

* Candidates for confirmation are then presented to the bishop by the pastor or catechist (*Rite of Confirmation*, 21). The one presenting them speaks in his or her own words, announcing these individuals as heirs to the gift of the risen Lord, his own Spirit.

* Each is called by name, if numbers allow for this. (This reminds the candidate and the assembly that God calls each of us by name to a life of faith.)

Homily

The homily will be affected by the quality of the planners' reflections on the liturgy and the scriptures during the preparation process.

* The results of this reflection process should be shared with the homilist.

* The homilist is not confined to the sample
   homily in the rite (#22).

* The candidates are seated, and the presider
   gives a brief homily addressed first of all to
   the entire assembly, but also to the candidates.

Renewal of Baptismal Promises

* Rehearse this profession of faith with the
   candidates so that it will be a strong and
   significant moment.

* The candidates alone stand for this, and
   they alone respond to the questions from
   the presider.

* Then the bishop and the whole assembly
   "confirms their profession of faith" either
   through a proclamation of the bishop
   ("This is our faith . . ."), or by a hymn
   or acclamation sung by everyone. (This
   profession of faith replaces the normal reci-
   tation of the creed at this liturgy.)

Laying on of Hands

The bishop calls everyone to pray that the Father pour
out the Spirit on these sons and daughters and make them
more Christlike. All pray in silence; the laying on of
hands follows. Then the bishop, in the name of all, sings

the prayer of consecration over the candidates. The prayer of consecration may also be recited.

The number of candidates will affect how the laying on of hands is done. If there are few candidates, there can be more flexibility in the arrangements.

If sponsors, parents and family groups are to lay hands on the candidates while the bishop extends hands over all during the prayer of consecration

* the bishop's invitation to prayer should instruct them to gather around the candidates

* they should lay hands on the candidates' heads as the time of silent prayer begins and throughout the prayer of consecration

* the bishop should allow an adequate time for silent prayer

If the candidates are to process to the ministers for the laying on of hands and the number of candidates is small

* they should come forward one at a time

* they should remain in place throughout the anointing

If the bishop (assisted by priests who are concelebrants) will lay hands on the candidates individually

* this takes place during the time of silent prayer

* ministers and candidates should be positioned so that the gesture is visible to all

* candidates can come forward to the ministers one at a time or ministers may move to the place(s) where the candidates are standing

* the prayer of consecration should not begin until the laying on of hands is completely finished so that full attention can be given to the solemn prayer of consecration

If the ministers will simply extend their hands over all the candidates at once, this gesture is done during the time of silent prayer and continues during the prayer of consecration.

Anointing with Chrism

The container of chrism is carried to the bishop; small bowls and towels for each anointing minister are brought to him from a side table. The chrism is carefully poured into the small containers. The bishop may pray a prayer of thanksgiving for the chrism at this time. The bishop then hands the chrism to each of the assisting ministers, symbolically delegating them to anoint.

The sponsor stands with the candidate and places a hand on his or her shoulder during the anointing. The minister rubs a generous amount of chrism onto each candidate's forehead saying, "N., be sealed with the Gift of the Holy Spirit." The candidate responds, "Amen." The scented oil is left on the forehead, not wiped off. Then the minister says, "Peace be with you," (the greeting of the risen Lord to his followers) to which the candidate replies, "And also with you."

This action should be done without song or musical accompaniment. The assembly should remain seated.

Plans for this anointing include arranging

* where this might take place so that all can hear and see easily

* how the ministers will be given the candidates' names

* where the ministers may clean their hands after the anointing

General Intercessions

As the Spirit is poured out upon us for the sake of the world, so we close this rite by praying with Christ for the church and the world.

* Everyone stands for these prayers.

* The intercessions are best sung as a litany, with cantor singing the intention and everyone the response.

* If the prayers are recited, be clear who is to lead them, "deacon or minister" (#30). Even if the intentions are spoken, the assembly may still sing the response.

Liturgy of the Eucharist

The liturgy of the eucharist is the culmination of the sacraments of initiation and of this liturgy. In preparation, be mindful of

* including some of the newly confirmed in the procession with the gifts and the preparation of the altar

* asking some of the candidates or their parents to bake the unleavened bread for this sacred meal

* singing the acclamations of the eucharistic prayer

* preparing a sufficient number of communion ministers for an orderly preparation of the bread and wine, and for a gracious and timely sharing of communion

* ensuring that the assembly is invited to receive both the eucharistic bread and the cup

* providing a simple, joyful refrain or song during the communion procession

The liturgy concludes with a solemn blessing or a prayer over the people (#33), which replaces the usual blessing.

Suggested Readings

These books will be helpful to those involved in the parish's preparations for confirmation. The list includes books referred to in this work and other titles as well. They provide valuable insights on liturgy and sacraments in general and on confirmation in particular. The books listed are readily available and are suggested for parish staff members, those preparing for the liturgy, catechists and other interested people.

Gerard Austin. *Anointing with the Spirit: The Rite of Confirmation. The Use of Oil and Chrism.* Collegeville: Pueblo Publishing Co./The Liturgical Press, 1985.

Annibale Bugnini. *The Reform of the Liturgy, 1948–1975.* Collegeville: The Liturgical Press, 1990. (See chapter 37, "Confirmation," pages 613–625.)

J. D. Crichton. *Christian Celebration: The Sacraments.* London: Geoffrey Chapman, 1973.

Tad Guzie. *The Book of Sacramental Basics.* New York: Paulist Press, 1981.

Aidan Kavanagh. *The Shape of Baptism: The Rite of Christian Initiation.* Collegeville: Pueblo Publishing Co./The Liturgical Press, 1978.

Aidan Kavanagh. *Confirmation: Origins and Reform.* Collegeville: Pueblo Publishing Co./The Liturgical Press, 1988.

Lambert Leijssen, ed. "Confirmation: Origins, History and Pastoral Situation Today." In *Questions Liturgiques*, vol. 70 (1989, 1–2). Proceedings of the VIIIth International Colloquium on Liturgy held at Louvain, Belgium. Louvain, Belgium: Liturgisch Institut.

John Roberto. *Confirmation in the American Catholic Church.* A 1978 NCDD Resource Paper. Washington: National Conference of Diocesan Directors of Religious Education, 1978.

Mark Searle. *Christening: The Making of Christians.* Collegeville: The Liturgical Press, 1980.

———. *The Church Speaks about Sacraments with Children: Baptism, Confirmation, Eucharist, Penance.* Chicago: Liturgy Training Publications, 1990.

Alternative Futures for Worship, Vol. 2: Baptism and Confirmation. Edited by Mark Searle. Collegeville: The Liturgical Press, 1987.

Paul Turner. *Confirmation: The Baby in Solomon's Court.* New York: Paulist Press, 1993.

———. *Sources of Confirmation: From the Fathers through the Reformers.* Collegeville: The Liturgical Press, 1993.